Icarus World Issues Series

Teenage Soldiers
Adult Wars

Series Editors, Roger Rosen and Patra McSharry

THE ROSEN PUBLISHING GROUP, INC.
NEW YORK

Published in 1991 by The Rosen Publishing Group, Inc.
29 East 21st Street, New York, NY 10010

Copyright 1991 by The Rosen Publishing Group, Inc.

First Edition

Library of Congress Cataloging-in-Publication Data
Teenage soldiers, adult wars.—1st ed.
      p.   cm.—(Icarus world issues series)
   Includes bibliographical references and index.
   Summary: A collection of fictional and non-fictional stories and essays dealing with war and its effects on the young.
   ISBN 0-8239-1304-X (hardcover)
   ISBN 0-8239-1305-8 (paperback)
   1. War—Literary collections.
  [1. War—Literary collections.]
  I. Rosen Publishing Group.   II. Series.
PZ5. T2944   1991
808.8'0358—dc20   90-26638
                                                           CIP
                                                            AC

Manufactured in the United States of America

CONTENTS

Introduction iv

We Will Remember 1
Tatyana Ivnitskaya

In the Clearing 17
Robert Olen Butler

A Slight Deception 27
Yitzhak Ben-Ner

Taking Liberties: The Lithuanian Exodus 43
from the Soviet Army
Liudvika Vildziunaite-Pociuniene

X. M. G. 59
Aly Renwick

Nicaragua in Black and White: Images 77
of a Generation Marked by War
Michael Williamson

A Sound of Drowning Pebbles 103
Bruce Moore-King

The Cemetery 113
Christine H. Dabague

Tienanmen Square: A Soldier's Story 129
Xiao Ye

A Line in the Sand 141
Fr. Kevin Dowling

Vladek and the Clown 151
Piotr Stasinski

Glossary 164

Bibliography 165

Index 169

Introduction

Welcome to the premiere volume in the *Icarus World Issues Series*. *Icarus* was conceived as an expression of Rosen Publishing's passionate commitment to developing citizens of the world. It is a commitment founded on the conviction that a safer planet and a more compassionate, concerned individual will inevitably arise from a greater understanding of the thoughts and longings of peoples throughout the world. The *Icarus* series exists to foster that greater understanding.

We regard each book in the series as our North American home where we play host to an international group of writers and photographers. Their varied points of view on given issues diverge in every way except the originality with which they are expressed. Just as we offer them the metaphoric armchair and cup of coffee, so too do we invite you, the reader, to join us. We will be much surprised if you don't find our living room the most remarkable into which you have ever ventured. Where else could you find a Pulitzer Prize winner just back from Nicaragua hobnobbing with a Chinese dissident plagued by the memory of the events in Tienanmen Square? Or bump into a U.S. Air Force chaplain eager to relate his experiences in Saudi Arabia with Operation Desert Shield? Or hear from one of Israel's most respected novelists? Those are just a few of the contributors waiting to engage you here in a thought-provoking discourse on some of the pressing issues of the day.

The story behind our first volume, **Teenage Soldiers, Adult Wars**, may not measure up to Homer's definition of an Odyssey, but it certainly gave us in the editorial department a run for our money.

Not long ago, when many international observers were talking about how the end of the Cold War would soon bring a peace dividend to be enjoyed by everyone, I was flying back from Moscow with a reasonably optimistic attitude about our collective chances for survival. The idea to create *Icarus* was already fairly well defined, and my recent meetings with many Russian writers and journalists convinced me that the logistics for a book series that brought together artists from around the world were distinctly workable. (The fax machine has changed all our lives.) On the flight I was casting about for a topic for the first volume. It had to be one that would immediately resonate with students everywhere. In my mind, war suggested itself, then receded; other issues such as student strikes and activism in general came forward. But the theme of war didn't go away. Wars have always been fought by you, the young, you of draft age wherever you may be—young patriots or cannon fodder, depending on one's point of view. And the cost of war has always been so very great, and the soldier's knowledge going into war perhaps not as complete as one would hope.

Back in New York, I switched on the news and heard that young Lithuanian soldiers had deserted from the Soviet Army and fled to their homeland which had just recently declared its independence. Many of these young men were later seized by a crack Soviet paratrooper unit and taken away. To where? Many of us wanted to know, especially our editorial department. We started looking for an answer. Through various channels, we commissioned Liudvika Vildziunaite-Pociuniene, a member of the Lithuanian Parliament's special commission on Lithuanian soldiers, to write an exclusive article on their fate.

At this time, we also became acquainted with the most recent book by Israel's prize-winning novelist Yitzhak Ben-Ner. It recounts the story of a young Israeli soldier forced to patrol the occupied territories during the time of the *intifada*. The promise of peace began to seem more and more illusory. We asked to see an English translation of the first chapter and marveled at the poignancy of the story.

And so it went: Stories and essays arrived on our desks from country after war-torn country. Sometimes the tragic events had occurred some years earlier, as in Robert Olen Butler's story about the war in Vietnam; sometimes the event was, in fact, on the verge of happening, as in Father Kevin Dowling's firsthand report on the Persian Gulf.

We soon had the makings of our first volume. Grim, hauntingly beautiful, at times even strangely funny, **Teenage Soldiers**, **Adult Wars** is a unique volume of writing and photoessays about youth living in the shadow of conflict. We are confident that you will find it as compelling as we do.

Roger Rosen, Publisher

WE WILL
REMEMBER

TATYANA IVNITSKAYA

Tatyana Ivnitskaya is a Soviet journalist who attended the School of Journalism at Moscow State University. She was married to Andrei Nasedkin, who also enrolled at the university but was subsequently expelled. Thereafter he was drafted into the Soviet Army and served in Afghanistan.

After he returned from his period of duty, he described his experiences of the war in Afghanistan to Ms. Ivnitskaya, who recorded and transcribed them. Following are two of the memories he recounted to her shortly before his death.

Dmitrii Likhanov attended the School of Journalism concurrently with Ms. Ivnitskaya. He is the publisher of the Russian-language journal *Top Secret*, in which this article first appeared.

Both Ms. Ivnitskaya and Mr. Likhanov live in Moscow.

Photo by Artem Borovik

*A*ctually, everybody called him Sed. Even his wife and close friends. It was more stylish and just shorter that way. His real name was Andrei Nasedkin and he was our classmate, a hooligan and a clown.

Nasedkin became Sed during the first autumn of our college years, when the university administration sent us to help the farmers gather the harvest. For more than two months we waded through the frigid soil in our heavy boots, following the tractor and picking up the already frozen potatoes. In the evenings, exhausted and dirty, we would return to the plywood barracks of the nearest children's summer camp. And suddenly, when it seemed that nothing in this cold, wet world could bring enthusiasm back into our lives, we heard Sed's hoarse voice. He was singing a song about Montana.

When we were in our third year the war began. Soon after that, Sed showed up in a military uniform. We were standing around, and I remember his saying, "That's it, guys, I've had enough. I'm going to Afghanistan. Maybe it'll be great . . . "

At that time we still didn't know what "Afghanistan" really meant. He wasn't killed. I think he wasn't even wounded. He returned alive and physically unharmed. But completely different. He didn't sing about Montana anymore. He only drank. And shot up like a demon.

Two years ago they found him in a bathtub with his wrists slashed. No one knew why he did this to himself. Some said that he had overdosed. I thought so too at first. Until I read Sed's stories, recorded in writing by Tatyana Ivnitskaya.

Then many things became clear. It became clear why he returned a different person, and why he couldn't live as if

3

nothing had happened, as if there were no Afghanistan, no blood, no deaths.

You could say that Sed was unfortunate. After all, war didn't finish him off in a dusty foxhole in Afghanistan or in an ambush during an attack on an Afghan village. It finished him off in a bathroom, to the music of "Deep Purple" and the smell of cologne. You can't say that he died like a hero. So I am not going to talk about heroism. But I think his death was an honest one. But it's useless to talk about it now . . .

The Dream

"What are you screaming about?"

Mishka elbowed me in the ribs. It was humid in the tent, humid and sticky, like a sauna. Covered with sweat, I was lying in bed and wondering whether I was awake.

"What are you screaming about?" Mishka repeated, squeezing my hand.

Our cots stood side by side, touching. He pulled my hand strongly, and then I really woke up.

"I had a stupid dream," I whispered. Mishka knew about this dream, but then he knew a lot about me in general. Sometimes that's good—that way you never have to explain. My hands were swollen. So were my feet and my whole body, but especially the hands. My fists were clenched so tightly that my fingers were numb.

"It's okay," Mishka whispered in my ear, "I dreamt about my first, too." He sighed. We were silent. He had guessed correctly.

I had dreamt about my "first."

"Mishka, let's have a smoke. Just a couple of drags?" I suggested indecisively. Chills were slowly beginning to shake my body. It was almost ironic in the unbearable heat. Mishka nodded. It's always like this: Even though I know I shouldn't, I always turn him on to some unhealthy nonsense. Of course, I try to "battle the evil within" and all that—"not risking my health," as our ensign puts it. But this stupid dream is going to be the end of me someday. I hate myself for having it, but it happens anyway.

I inhaled deeply a few times and got sort of warmer and drier. Calmer, too. Improved my health, you might say. Ha! I feel so bad I could shoot myself right now. Aaah. Well, isn't he the nervous, sensitive type. "Journalist." "Moscow." They started calling me that from the beginning. The commander coined the nicknames, and they stuck. I closed my eyes and tried to relax. I was afraid to fall asleep: Sometimes the dream came two or three times in one night. Maybe you never become used to it.

We had just been transferred. Already trained, but still inexperienced in combat. We were standing in the shadow of some building without a roof, not really knowing why. We stood at ease, relaxed, but a little restless. Sergeant Lyashko was sitting on an empty Japanese beer box and biting his nails. The day was uncomfortably bright, and we were all waiting for something to happen. In my dream, it is always an early, overcast morning, and I always know what is going to happen next.

Finally, they brought them. Their hands were tied behind their backs, and frankly, they looked pretty pathetic. It seemed impossible, unfathomable, that these boys were the enemy. Except for two older men, all of them appeared to be our age or younger. Our platoon commander appeared from somewhere and explained to us what an enemy is and how we were to deal with him. He also said something about the counterrevolution and about the homefront that must be protected at all costs.

But they just stood there with their bound hands, looking as pitiful as sparrows. One of them caught my eye, this boy who kept staring at me and smiling in a fawning kind of way. I don't know for sure; maybe I imagined it.

But I definitely felt a kind of connection, as if I wanted to speak to him or something. I couldn't possibly convince myself that this was "the enemy who had to be destroyed." Suddenly it began—the "disposal," a test of sorts. One by one they were placed with their backs to us against the wall of the insane roofless building. The sergeant, biting his nails, shouted out a name. The soldier who was called would come forward and fire at the boy who stood against the wall. Unfortunately, this wasn't a nightmare but a reality and—worse than that—an order. When my turn came, the sergeant stopped biting his nails for a moment, smiled kind of sarcastically, and yelled: "Come on, Journalist!"

I don't know what my face could have looked like, but I felt a tremor shake my body, and something inside me suddenly came undone. I understood now that I had to kill this unarmed boy with his hands tied behind his back, and for some reason he was the same one who had looked into my eyes with that strange smile. To kill him. Not knowing why or for what. I don't think he understood. Not until the very end.

I raised my machine gun, convinced that this couldn't be happening and never would. Never. I had to—just had to—wake up in my own house on Begovaya Street in Moscow, in my own bed, with my wife or without her— the hell with her. I just had to wake up.

With my gray eyes, I looked into his smooth, black, buttery eyes. He didn't understand. All this lasted for a moment, maybe a fraction of a second, but in my dream it lasts entire nights. Finally he understood something. Maybe it was the word "Journalist," because I thought I saw something like a smile on his face. He probably thought that this was all a mistake, a misunderstanding, that everything would turn out well, and that maybe we could meet and become friends and he could invite me to his house...

He must have thought that, because he even took a step in my direction as if he wanted to say something. I lowered the barrel of my gun and sighed, almost in relief.

I was pulled back into the nightmare by Lyashko's scream: "Hey, Moscow! What're you, asleep?"

I raised the gun once again. I no longer understood anything.

"Comrade Sergeant Lyashko! Please permit me to untie his hands!" I said in a completely unmilitary fashion, with a tongue that felt dry and alien in my mouth.

"Are you crazy, Journalist? Carry out the order! Bayonet him! Come on!"

"Don't, please don't! Lyashko, sergeant, darling, don't," I wanted to yell. I wanted to scream, crawl around on my hands and knees and kiss Lyashko's dusty American boots. But for some reason my voice quietly answered: "Yes, sir! Bayonet him, sir!" Maybe someone needed it to happen this way, I don't know, maybe. But once again I dream about his smile, his eyes, his voice with its strange melodious accent. He never did turn his back to me.

"I am a student! I am twenty-one, you see? I am a journalist. So why? Why? What for? I am a student, I've got a mother!"*

Of course, we were taught. We were taught to kill in all possible and impossible ways. But it took six blows for me to kill him. The bayonet kept hitting his ribs, his breastbone, his collarbone. It must have hurt him terribly, probably even more than it hurt me.

He lay still, his eyes open wide with disbelief. His mouth was open too, and dark blood was already streaming out of it in a twisted path.

---

* Italicized portions were originally written in English.

"Bad, very bad," remarked Lyashko disapprovingly, "and a straight A student, too. All right, wipe off your snot..." Then he yelled, "Krasilshikov, use your bayonet!" and winked at me cunningly, saying: "Learn, student! Mos-cow."

I really didn't have any snot on my face, or any vomit either. I had simply killed a person, maybe even a very good one. Maybe I had killed two people, if you count me.

It's just that this stupid dream won't go away. And Mishka says that for some reason in my dream I keep yelling: "*I am twenty-one! I am a student! You see? You believe?*"

Although in six days, if I don't get killed, I'm going to be twenty-two.

Photo by Artem Borovi

Photo by Artem Borovik

Photo by Artem Borovik

My Dear Son

For a long time after receiving the letter I couldn't figure out who it was from. I thought I'd received it by mistake, but my name was written on the envelope and the letter called me by my name. After reading through half of it, I finally figured it out. I thought I must have been dreaming when I realized that the letter had been sent by Mishka's mother. I didn't finish reading it, and instead went out behind the tent, where an assortment of charred cups, empty condensed milk cans, and other garbage was piled in a heap. I just sat there, looking at our huge tent and all the others just like it. They are exactly the same color as the sand of Registan, this godforsaken desert. It's a strange coincidence. But there are really no coincidences in this world.

It seems that I am remembering Samarkand, where my father and I used to go about ten years ago. I was a snot-nosed kid then, so small that I could walk under the table. Well, I am exaggerating, of course, but I definitely remember the desert. In Ulukbek, the religious academy had a teahouse and herons nested on the roofs of the old mosques. Why am I remembering all of this now? I am tired of thinking about the dunes, the tumbleweed, the "white sun of the desert," and the 60°C heat. I am just tired of thinking. That's why I am sitting here smoking weed and why I am taking a hit of opium. Damn, it's bitter! It'd be nice to wash it down with something. I wonder if I've got any water left? I shake the canteen and determine what's left by the sound: not even a full swallow. And it's really hitting me now, too. My eyes are getting hot, and my arms and legs are getting cold. I lie down on my side in the shadow of this orange tent. My teeth are grinding sand. I look at my hands: They are the color of chocolate, and the hair is no longer golden, but pure white, like old people's hair. Does body hair turn white? I'll ask the platoon commander, he knows everything. Why is this crap running through my head?!

I start to laugh, not really knowing why. I don't want to laugh. I am terrified of the platoon commander, afraid of him with every fiber of my being. He's really an excellent guy . . . Why am I laughing?

I take the carefully folded letter out of my pocket and start to read again. Why is it written in green ink? Before it was written in blue. Right in front of my eyes, it becomes red. This is what I read: "My dear son!" . . . And again, I feel the lump in my throat; again the tears; and the dryness in my throat, the miserable dryness in my throat. Isn't the opium working? I am crying, I am hurting, I close my eyes and see a red and green haze. It is the sun. It is the color of my eyelids—in them, through tiny capillaries, blood is flowing. The holiday of Ramadan . . . I am a drug addict . . . I am a soldier, or rather, a professional killer. We are called "Shuravi-Hitlers"* by the peaceful locals or the Dushmans**—but who can tell them apart? All their faces merge into one.

Pictures begin to flicker under my closed eyelids . . . "My dear son!" . . . I see a road. With a strange roar, armored cars move down the road. I am a gun layer and operator, a marksman. We are all covered with red dust, which is clay. It's very soft to the touch, like powder or flour. We pass the armored car from Kandagar. Mishka is in the first one, I am in the second. In the third there's a correspondent from some Moscow newspaper. Platoon commander Dzyuba is there, too. And Letunovskii is with them: his heroic chest stuck out, lined with medals, his

---

*Shuravi-Hitler—Afghan term meaning killer.
**Dushman—Soviet term for Afghan fighters.

machine gun hanging down and his beret cocked to the side—he doesn't wear a helmet. He will go home soon; he's almost demobilized. In the first armored car there's Mishka, my "countryman"—we're both from Elektrostal. I know everything about him and about Lenka, his girlfriend; I even know that soon he's going to be a father.

I open my eyes, wanting this movie to end. I've seen it already. I don't want to see it again. I have been seeing this movie for half a year now, and it's enough! My eyes rest on the blindingly white paper of the letter. Mishka's mother wrote it. Dammit, but she doesn't know anything. And she'll never find out . . .

Somebody is behind me: it's "Macaroni" Klotchkov, our pathetic ensign. "Verevkin, are you risking your health again?" he asks. He is talking to me. I really want to "gas" him, but it's so hot that I feel lazy. So I answer calmly, "Yes, sir, Comrade Macaroni, I am risking my health, sir." And I exhale smoke, kind of nonchalantly, so that it looks as if I am not releasing it right into his face, but somewhere upward, into the sky or something. Into the sky of Registan. He screams something, but I just open one eye and stare at his ugly, brutal face. Everything seems funny again, but I don't have enough energy to laugh or stand up. I take another deep drag and focus my eyes on the white triangle of the letter. No, it's a rectangle. This is unbearable . . . I close my eyes and hear the roar of the engine. Mishka and a few others are first. Toliberdiev, myself, and Ostratyuk are behind them and Samoilov, Letunovskii, the correspondent, and Dzyuba bring up the rear.

Once again, my hands become cold and a lump forms in my throat. My heart, it seems, stops beating for a moment. I see everything as in a silent film, except that instead of being in black and white it is in green and red. I see Mishka's armored car explode. It's a good distance away, and Toliberdiev has time to slam on the brakes. We skid and I jump out. I am running. I am running to Mishka, running, running. But for some reason, I remain in one place. This often happens in dreams. Samoilov is running, the correspondent is running, Dzyuba is running, Toliberdiev is running. Only Letunovskii is lying on the side of the road, a large black-red stain spreading on his heroic chest. Someone says the word "shrapnel." His beret is still on his head, and his blond forelock is waving in the wind. And he was due to go home soon! Everything around is slowly swaying. I am running. Someone is pulling Mishka out of the wreck, but for some reason he has no legs. He is lying on the road in the red dust, and next to him something bluish and semitransparent is lying in a red puddle. Mishka frantically turns his head side to side and I know he's looking for me.

"I am here! Mishka, Mishka, I am here, do you hear me?" I scream into his ear.

I understand that he's alive, but like me, he probably can't hear anything at all. I tear open my first aid kit and give Mishka an injection. Then I lie down next to him on the road; all kinds of strange legs are surrounding us. All the boots are covered with red dust. And I notice that the bluish, mother-of-pearl–tinged heap is also covered w .n the dust. It turns different colors, and something in it moves, pulsates. I become frightened. Terrified. I think Mishka also understands that this heap is his intestines.

He soundlessly moves his absolutely white lips, trying to say something to me, and I put my ear against his mouth. "Volodya!" I hear him whisper, as though from a great distance, "Dear Volodya, shoot me! Shoot me in the head! Shoot already, you bastard!" And suddenly it dawns on me, I understand everything and scream—the silent movie ends. I scream as hard as I can with my parched throat, with my dust-choked lungs, I simply scream, "A-a-ah!" I don't hear the shot. I fall on Mishka, my chest against his, screaming hysterically. Clutching my machine gun, I aim at everybody around us. I see the formless heap still moving. And then I hear the click of a camera shutter.

Someone kicks the machine gun out of my hands, probably just in time. I don't remember what happened after that. It was very hot. They say that I attacked the correspondent and that they had to pull me away while I was violently thrashing and kicking, trying to crush the camera that had fallen into the dust. They say I even decked Dzyuba a couple of times. I guess these things happen sometimes.

I was sent back to Elektrostal along with Mishka. There we were met by his mother, Lenka, and his newborn son, also named Mishka.

Here the movie ends. I lied to his mother, I lied to Lenka, I got disgustingly drunk and cried, and lied all the time, afraid to stop. About battle, about demonic Dushmans, about exploding bullets, blasts, shrapnel, and nightly parachute jumps. And about some incredible act of heroism performed by Mishka. I lied because I had to. I had to for them.

And so I receive a letter. I can't write back, even though I know that Mishka was an only child and that his mother had only asked me to let her call me "my dear son." But I never read the letter to the end. I couldn't. Maybe I lost my mind from this sweltering heat, or from the weed and opium. I threw the letter into the garbage heap of old cans and watched it burn slowly. I have this great American lighter which, back then, during our trip to Termeza, I swapped with Mishka for a badge that said "100 jumps."

Translated by Alex Halberstadt

IN THE CLEARING

ROBERT OLEN BUTLER

Robert Olen Butler was born in Granite City, Illinois. He attended Northwestern University and received an M.A. in playwriting at the University of Iowa. In 1971 he served in Vietnam as a Vietnamese linguist for the U.S. Army.

He has written six novels, *The Alleys of Eden, Sun Dogs, Countrymen of Bones, On Distant Ground, Wabash*, and *The Deuce*. In 1987 he won the Tu Do Chinh Kien Award, sponsored by the Vietnam Veterans of America, for outstanding contribution to American culture.

Mr. Butler teaches creative writing at McNeese State University, Lake Charles, Louisiana. He is currently preparing a screenplay for *The Alleys of Eden*.

The following selection is from his forthcoming book, *A Good Scent from a Strange Mountain*. The book, a collection of short stories, some of which have appeared in publications such as the *Hudson Review*, the *Southern Review*, and the *Virginia Quarterly*, is scheduled for publication by Simon & Schuster in the fall of 1991.

Mr. Butler lives in Lake Charles, Louisiana, with his wife and son.

Though I have never seen you, my son, do not think that I am unable to love you. You were in your mother's womb when the North of our country took over the South and some of those who fought the war found themselves running away. I did not choose to run, not with you ready to enter this world. I did not choose to leave my homeland and become an American. I have chosen so few of the things of my life, really. I was eighteen when Saigon was falling and you were dreaming on in your little sea inside your mother in a thatched house in An Khe. Your mother loved me then and I loved her and I would not have left except I had no choice. This has always been a strange thing to me, though I have met several others here where I live in New Orleans, Louisiana, who are in the same condition. It is strange because I know how desperately many others wanted to get out, even hiding in the landing gears of the departing airplanes. I myself had not thought of running away, did not choose to, but it happened to me anyway.

I am sorry. And I write you now not to distract you from your duty to your new father, as I am sure your mother would fear. I write with a full heart for you because I must tell you a few things about being a person who is somewhere between a boy and a man. I was just such a person when I held a rifle in my hands. It was a black thing, the M16 rifle, black like a charcoal cricket, and surprisingly light, with a terrible voice, a terrible quick voice like the river demons my own father told stories about when it was dark and nighttime in our village and I wanted to be frightened.

That is one thing I must tell you. As a boy you wish to be frightened. You like the night; you like the quickness inside you as you and your friends speak of mysterious things, ghosts and spirits, and you wish to go out into the dark and go as far down the forest path as you can without turning back. You and your friends go down the path together and no one dares to say that you have gone too far even though you hear every tiny sound from the darkness around you and these sounds make you quake inside. Am I right about this? I dream of you often and I can see you in this way with your friends and it is the same as it was with me and my friends.

This is all right, to embrace the things you fear. It is natural and it will help build the courage you must have as a man. But when you are a man, don't become confused. Do not seek out the darkness, the things you fear, as you have done as a boy. This is not a part of you that you should hold on to. I myself did not hold on to it for more than a few minutes once the rifle in my hand heard the cries of other rifles calling it. I no longer dream of those few minutes. I dream only of you.

I cannot remember clearly now any of the specific moments of my real fear, of my man's fear with no delight in it at all, no happiness, no sense of power or of my really deep down controlling it, of being able to turn back with my friends and walk out of the forest. I can only remember a wide rice paddy and the air leaning against me like a drunken man who says he knows me and I remember my boots full of water and always my thought to check to see if I was wrong, if there was really blood in my boots, if I had somehow stepped on a mine and been too scared to even realize it and I was walking with my boots filled with blood. But this memory is the sum of many moments like these. All the particular rice paddies and tarmac highways and hacked jungle paths—the exact, specific ones—are gone from me.

Only this remains. A clearing in a triple canopy mahogany forest in the Highlands. The trees were almost a perfect circle around us and in the center of the clearing was a large tree that had been down for a long time. We were a patrol and we were sitting in a row against the dead trunk, our legs stuck out flat or tucked up to our chests. We were all young and none of us knew what he was doing. Maybe we were stupid for stopping where we did. I don't know about that.

But our lieutenant let us do it. He was sitting on the tree trunk, his elbows on his knees, leaning forward smoking a cigarette. He was right next to me and I knew he wanted to be somewhere else. He was pretty new, but he seemed to know what he was doing. His name was Linh and he was maybe twenty-one, but I was eighteen and he seemed like a man and I was a private and he was our officer, our platoon leader. I wanted to speak to him because I was feeling the fear pretty bad, like it was a river catfish with the sharp gills and it was just now pulled out of the water and into the boat, thrashing, with the hook still in its mouth, and my chest was the bottom of the boat.

I sat trying to think what to say to Lieutenant Linh, but there was only a little nattering in my head, no real words at all. Then another private sitting next to me spoke. I do not remember his name. I can't shape his face in my mind anymore. Not even a single feature. But I remember his words. He lifted off his helmet and placed it on the ground beside him and he said, "I bet no man has ever set his foot in this place before."

I heard Lieutenant Linh make a little snorting sound at this, but I didn't pick up on the contempt of it or the bitterness. I probably would've kept silent if I had. But instead, I said to the other private, "Not since the dragon came south."

Lieutenant Linh snorted again. This time it was clear to both the other soldier and me that the lieutenant was responding to us. We looked at him and he said to the other, "You're dead meat if you keep thinking like that. It's probably too late for you already. There've been men in this place before, and you better hope it was a couple of days ago instead of a couple of hours."

We both turned our faces away from the rebuke and my cheeks were hotter than the sun could ever make them, even though the lieutenant had spoken to the other private. But I was not to be spared. The lieutenant tapped me on the shoulder with iron fingertips. I looked back to him and he bent near with his face hard, like what I'd said was far worse than the other.

He said, "And what was that about the dragon?"

I was too frightened now to make my mind work. I could only repeat, "The dragon?"

"The dragon," he said, his face coming nearer still. "The thing about the dragon going south."

For a moment I felt relieved. I don't know how the lieutenant sensed this about me, but somehow he knew that when I spoke of the dragon going south it was not just a familiar phrase meant to refer to a long time ago. He knew that I actually believed. But at that moment I did not understand how foolish this made me seem to him. I said, "The dragon. You know, the gentle dragon who was the father of Vietnam."

The story my father told of the gentle dragon and the fairy princess had always been different from the ones about ghosts that I sought in the candlelight to chill me, though my father did believe in ghosts, as do many Vietnamese people and even some Americans. But the story of how our country began was always told in the daylight and with many of our family members gathered together, and no one ever said to me that this was just a made-up story, that this was just a lovely little lie. When I studied American history to become a citizen here, there was a story of a man named George Washington and he cut down a little tree and then told the truth. And the teacher immediately told us that this was just a made-up story. He made this very clear for even something like that. Just cutting down a tree and telling the truth about it. We had to keep that story separate from the stories that were actual true history.

This makes me sad about this country that was chosen for me. It makes me sad for a whole world of adults. It makes me sad even for Lieutenant Linh as I remember his questions that followed, all with a clenched face and a voice as quick and furious as the rifles at our sides. "Is this the dragon who slept with the fairy?" he demanded, though the actual words he used at that moment of my own true history were much harsher.

"He married a fairy princess," I said.

"Who married them?" the lieutenant said.

I couldn't answer the question. It was a simple question and it was, I see now, an unimportant question, but sitting in that clearing in the middle of a forest full of men who would kill me, having already fired my rifle at their shapes on several occasions and felt the rush of their bullets past my face and seen already two men die, though I turned my face from that, but having seen two men splashed with their own blood and me sitting now in a forest with the fear clawing at my chest, I faced that simple little question and I realized how foolish I was, how much a child.

The lieutenant cried, "Is this the fairy princess who's going to *lay eggs?*"

And in a moment as terrible as when I first felt the fear of my adult self, I now turned my face from the lieutenant and I looked across the clearing at the tree line and I knew that someone out there was coming near and I knew that dragons and fairies do not have children and the lieutenant's voice was very close to me and it said, "Save your life."

I don't know if some time passed with me sitting there feeling as crumbly and dry as the tree trunk I leaned against. Maybe only a few seconds, maybe no seconds at all. But very soon, from the tree line before me, there was a flash of light and another and I could only barely shift my eyes to the private sitting next to me and his head was a blur of red and gray and I was as quick as my rifle and over the trunk and beside my lieutenant and we were very quiet together, firing, and all of the rest is very distant from me now. Half of our platoon was dead in those first few seconds, I think. When air support arrived, there was only the lieutenant and me and another private who would soon die from the wounds he received in those few minutes in the clearing.

Not many months later the lieutenant came to me where we were trying to dig in on the rim of Saigon and he said, "It's time." And all the troops of the Army of the Republic of Vietnam were streaming past us into the city, without leaders now, without hope, and so I followed Lieutenant Linh, I and a couple of other soldiers in his platoon that he knew were good fighters, and I did not understand exactly what he meant about its being time until we were in the motorboat of a friend of his and we were racing down the Saigon River. This was the last little bit of my childhood. I was holding my rifle across my chest, ready to fight wherever the lieutenant was leading me. But the lieutenant said, "You won't need that now."

He was taking me and the others into the South China Sea and when I realized I was leaving my country and my wife and my unborn son, I was only able to turn my face to him, for I knew there was no going back. He looked at me with a quick little smile, a warm smile, one man to another, and a nod of the head like he thought I was a good fighter, a good man, a man he respected, and all of that was true, and he thought he was helping me save my life, and maybe that was true, but maybe it wasn't true at all. You must understand, though, that I did not choose to leave.

My son, I love you. Your mother does not love me now and you have a new father. Has she told you about me?

Are you reading this? I pray you are; with all the little shiny pebbles of my childhood faith that I can find in the dust I pray it. And I am writing to tell you this. Thousands of years ago a gentle and kindly dragon grew lonely in the harsh wide plains of China and he wandered south. He found a land full of beautiful mountains and green valleys and fresh, clear rivers that ran so fast in their banks that they made a singing sound.

But even though the land was beautiful, he was still lonely. He traveled through this new country of his and at last he met a beautiful fairy princess. She, too, was lonely and the two of them fell in love and they decided to live together as man and wife and to love each other forever. And so they did live together in the beautiful land and one day the princess found that she had laid a hundred eggs in a beautiful silk pouch and these eggs hatched and they were the children of the dragon and the princess.

These children were very wonderful, inheriting bravery and gentleness from their father and beauty and charm and a delicacy of feeling from their mother. They grew and grew and they were fine, loving children but finally the dragon had to make a very difficult decision. He realized that the family was too large for them all to live together in one place. So he called his family to him and told them that even though he loved them all very much, he would have to divide the family into two parts. His wife would take fifty of the children and travel to the east. He would take the other fifty children and travel to the south. Everyone was very sad about having to do this, but they all understood that there was no other way.

So the princess took fifty of the children and went far away to the east where she became the Queen of the Ocean. And the dragon took fifty children far away to the south where he became the King of the Land. The dragon and the princess remained with the children until they were adults, wise and strong and able to take care of themselves. Then the dragon and the princess vanished and were reunited in the spirit world where they lived happily together for the rest of eternity. The children married and prospered and they created Vietnam from the far north to the southern tip and they are the ancestors of all of us. Of you, my son, and of me.

For a time in my life, the part of me that could believe in this story was dead. I often think, here in my new home, that it is dead still. But now, at least, I do not wish it to be dead and it does not make me feel foolish, so perhaps my belief is still part of me. I love you, my son, and all I wish for you is that you save your life. Tell this story that I have told you. Try to think of it as true.

A Slight
Deception

Yitzhak Ben-Ner

Y itzhak Ben-Ner was born in Kfar Yehoshua, Israel. He studied philosophy and literature in college. He is an award-winning novelist, film critic, journalist, screen-writer, and radio personality.

Mr. Ben-Ner is the author of *Protocol*, for which he won the Bernstein Prize, Israel's highest literary award, in 1983; *A Far Land*, for which he was awarded the Jerusalem Agnon Literary Award in 1982; and *A Rustic Sunset*, for which he received the Ramat Gan Award in 1979. He has also written children's books and short stories. Three of his short stories, "Atalia," "Winter Games," and "A Dime Novel," have been made into films.

Following is an excerpt from his most recent novel, *A Slight Deception*, published in Hebrew by Keter Publishing. This work is now being staged as a one-man performance in Israel. It recently won First Prize at the annual Monodrama Festival in Tel Aviv.

Mr. Ben-Ner lives in Tel Aviv with his wife and two children.

There was a kid there from the start. Yeah, of course there was a kid there. Just a second. That's important. That's real important. A matter of life or death. That's what I think. Don't know why. Anyway, after three weeks in that godawful city that Arab kid was just like one of the guys. Give me a minute to remember him, the little bastard: face like a donut, brownish. Eight or nine, say. Maybe less. How can you tell with them? My friend Etzion used to laugh at me and say that I wasn't the only juvenile in the platoon anymore. And Michel, he's the one from Ofakim, would always say then, like a joke, that he acts like a grown-up midget that the PLO disguised as a kid. He always had one of those knitted hats, blue and yellow stripes with a pompom on top, like I have in the picture with Mom when she was alive when I was three, and the hat is always sort of pulled down over his ears, and his straight brown hair always sticks out on the, you know, sides, from that beat-up cap. His name was Khaled ibn al-Zaim Houri—he would recite it, the whole name, like an answering machine, anytime one of the guys asked him, on purpose, just for kicks, out of boredom or whatever, Hey, kid, what's your name?—and he, tak tak tak, My name is Khaled-ibn-al-Zaim-Houri. We never saw Abu Khaled or Um Khaled, which is what they would call his dad and mom. They were probably scared to step out of the house and give him a smack on the face or yell at him and drag him back in, just like everyone else. Hey, there were hysterical mothers who would see their kids talking with us or bringing us gum, or walking behind us and saying Here's a terrorist house, here's a PLO house, and shouting Search! Search it!—anyway, we never saw Khaled's parents and he would walk along with us, on his own, almost—you know—running beside us to keep up on his little legs when we patrolled the streets. Maybe he didn't have any parents and his dad's name, al-Zaim, real or made-up, was all he had. Like a sort of identity card, I have my father's name, therefore I am. I don't know. But I had the feeling that someone, anyway, was taking care of the kid. 'Cause in the morning he would turn up with clean pants, always patched but always clean. It only took two or three hours for the jeans and the glow-in-the-dark blue wool sweater to get totally muddy and filthy. You know how filthy? You could see everywhere we had gone on them, all the streets and the alleys, every puddle, all the filth, every rock they threw at us that shattered a meter from our faces. It all stuck to him. Well, we were all filthy, too, and stank like rotting garbage. But that became more serious later.

Anyway, that kid, Khaled, would go everywhere with us. The little punk was really brave, wasn't scared of anything. Every morning when we came from the base for the patrol, the kid was already waiting for us, his sweater washed and dry and his pants clean and patched. He wouldn't even say hi, just straight off burst out talking a flood of Arabic that only Tali Salah could understand and translate for us. He says, Tali Salah would translate, that Husni and Daher and Mahmud, I guess they're his friends, he says each one got a shekel to throw stones at night at the guys from Platoon 2, the ones with the crew-cut sergeant. He means Sergeant Azarzar Zevik. Yeah, the bastard ratted on all his friends and was proud of it. Okay, he was only a kid and we were only kids, too, right?

Anyway, every morning was wet, sticky, lousy, you know—to be out like that at six-thirty in the morning, at a time yours truly didn't even used to know existed. After I finished school and exams, I wouldn't even go to bed until an hour or two before that, after a good night out on the town with the guys and my dad the worrier could finally get some sleep. And now, in the cold of the morning, this mist rises from the ground, and the water is still frozen, and fog and rain drizzles down from the sky like from the old gray canvas of the tent, and everyone is hunched over against the cold, feeling just like the weather. So we put our feet on autopilot and walk and, you know, drowse while we're walking, on both sides of the street, until the first rock or scream wakes us up. You walk and sleep, you know, wrapped up in your own little dream, not letting it leave you—and you hear all the guys drowsing on their feet, sleep-struck, you know, head lolling, bobbing, dragging along your red paratrooper's boots, bumping like that into the remains of yesterday's roadblocks—and only our corporal, Uzi Melamed, the kibbutznik, is, you know, on duty, keeping an eye out for our lives so they don't go to hell and trying to be alert and careful and look to both sides. So they don't surprise us. It's the regular route, that means from Feisal Street to Kasr-al-Houl Street and behind the military court in Palestine Square over there to that alley across from the police station and from there to the market and from there you go down to the southern kasbah and then you come out to Omar Street and go past the mosque and from there you climb up to their slums, by the graveyard, with the crazy lady that sits there at the gate and laughs and makes obscene gestures and cackles Go for it! at us, and from there along the wall of the high school and then you go back down into the refugee camp that the guys called the Pissistinian Transit Camp, and then the Prophet's Boulevard, the main mosque, the garages and all that and the mansions of the rich families with good connections, and then back to the city by way of the girls' school and the crowded houses there, and then back to Faraj Street, completing a circle. In the meantime, their muezzins start warbling from the minarets and wake up all the people who'll be throwing stones at you in a little while and those who'll curse at you and those who'll stare at you with such hatred, and the ones who keep their faces covered who, you know, run the show, tak tak tak, like by remote control, the riots and the women who start wailing afterwards. 'Cause all of them, and even the Shinbet* agents who try to hunt them down and interrogate them—they're all still sleeping just fine under their warm blankets when we start our morning patrol. We're the only ones out, dozing while we walk like schmucks, and that kid Khaled is with us and we go along for a while like that and only a few jittery early-bird storeowners rush to open their stores in the market and bring in some merchandise and sell something and make some money before the trouble starts and someone tells them to close and someone else tells them to open and all that.

The free-for-all begins afterwards. First cars begin filling the narrow streets, splitting your eardrums with their horns. You know, everything they've pent up inside them, those who don't dare to mess with us face to face, they take it out on each other by honking. Kids come out of the houses to go to school and stop at the first bend in the road, so their parents won't see them, and wait there to see what will happen—whatever is planned for the day. Sewage is already flowing down the little canals on the sides of the narrow, broken, battered roads, or in the dirt, twisting and turning until it flows into the stinking sewers. In the market, if there's no curfew on, you start seeing things move. It begins with smells. The smell of the fresh bread from Abu-Mazuz's big bakery really gets to you. The aroma of good coffee in the coffeehouse, where the first customers already sit by the plastic tables, looking at you with those, you know, far-off eyes, their faces blank, without expression. And then, if it's not raining, those old waiters begin going back and forth between the restaurants and the stores, carrying those huge trays with

---

*Shinbet—Israel's security agency.

one hand, mmmm, with *hummus* and *tahini* and olives and olive oil and the air, you know, fills with the smell of garlic and cumin and ground pepper and frying oil and cucumbers and tomatoes and, you know, fresh radishes that they cut into the salad. And we go by like that through those smells, geez, and wake up completely from our dreams and from—I don't know, from that sweet illusion and into the glare of the morning. Hey, we're not even allowed to dream of touching the stuff. You know, I'm up to here with money from my dad, who also plays mother to me, and I don't have anywhere to blow it. We're not allowed to have any contact with them. Can't buy squat. Not even a match. And they, you know, they certainly won't have anything to do with us. But Danny Peretz, who was there in the market once with his dad, when it was still quiet, except for a few stabbings here and there, says that their *hummus* tastes unreal. Then Etzion, the wise guy, says you know how much crap those Arabushes put in their *hummus*? Back in Israel, he says to make us feel better, spitting, in Israel no one touches *hummus* any more after what the television found out about what the Arab restaurant workers put into it. Got it? Okay, that stuff's what makes the best *hummus*, says Michel, and everyone laughs, except for our corporal whose eyes are skittering, you know, all around, from right to left, like one of those radars. Hey you, he says to Michel, I told you that I want the radio right behind me! So what are you dragging behind and opening your trap for? We talk at full volume because we're supposed to keep a safe distance from each other. On a patrol we walk, you know, three on each side of the street. It's best to walk under the awnings so that you don't get hit if they throw stones or bottles or potatoes stuck with nails or plastic bags full of piss. The first two, one of them the commander, walk with helmets on, the one next to the commander with a long-barreled Galil rifle that you can shoot tear gas or rubber bullet canisters with.

And everyone has a club except for that guy, you know, Yuval, the one from Ramat Hasharon who refuses to use one and the lieutenant told the corporals to let him alone. Anyway, the guy with the radio on his back walks behind the commander, and he carries ammunition and all sorts of other things. He's not much but a workhorse and it's not easy, so we all take turns doing it. Across from him is another one with extra ammo, helmets, and canteens for the guys. Those two stay behind to cover when everyone else runs forward to chase someone or whatever. In the back are two more, wearing flak jackets, so that no crazy guy with a knife jumps at them all of a sudden from some dark corner screaming *Allahu akbar** and all that.

Then the Border Patrol jeep is already there. The BPs make the Arabs quake. When we're, say, in the market and we pass by the chicken stalls or the butchers, those Arabs don't give a damn when we go by, they, you know, on purpose take a squawking chicken and, you know, lift it up, holding it by the head or by the comb with one hand like that—and with the other hand they draw the knife, on purpose, across the taut throat, just when we pass by them, and in a flash—they slash it and the blood, you know, spurts out and the body keeps jerking and they throw the head into the garbage pail next to them. So we should get the hint, the scum. And we can't do a thing to them. We just look and, you know, swallow hard and go on. Sometimes it makes your blood boil. Same with the nerve of the *shbab*, the teenage boys, who face you at a safe distance, maybe a hundred meters, throwing stones that don't hit you—because if they start hitting you, they know that you'll chase them—and shouting Hey, perverts, s.o.b.'s, and Slaughter the Jews. And sometimes they do karate, ninja, that kind of stuff, trying to provoke us,

---

* *Allahu akbar*—Arabic for "God is great."

calling us cowards or cursing our mothers. *Walla*, some-times you just want to bash their faces in. Anyway, to go back to those sonovabitch butchers, when we first came here we had this little guy, Ronny Fishler, who the guys would call Ronny Pisher, and the minute he saw that he straightaway bent over and puked. They laughed so hard, the scum, the slaughterers and butchers and chicken-men. The BPs don't do anything to them—but all of them, every one, you should see, freeze in fear when the Druze pass by. The whole BP really scares them stiff. Anyway, when the BP is there and all sorts of officers and civilians, like that friend of Dad's, Harul, start to walk around and check who opened and who didn't open their stores—'cause there are some there who get their orders from the PLO and all those about strikes and all that, and they don't open; and there are some who actually want to open, just to make a living, but they're scared to death of the PLO, who watch to make sure they don't open—so our job is so they'll know that we can scare them just as much as that Arafat, and so we go with the BPs to the stores where the metal shutter is pulled down and closed, or where there's a heavy iron door with a padlock, and we bang on the door and kick it and shout Hey, Abdallah, open the door! And the poor suckers hiding in the store, in the dark, behind the door, get scared we're going to break the windowpane or whatever, and they scream from inside, "Okay, okay, please, we open!" We shout in Arabic and they scream in English. Then we open it. Or the storeowners stand on the side, not far away, to see how things develop, and if they see that we're going to start breaking things they run up and start opening. 'Cause if they don't open up quietly, by themselves, what happens? We bring crowbars and we start to break in and if that doesn't help, there's always a car around with a welding machine that sometimes breaks the locks, when there's a commercial strike, and sometimes melts down locks on stores that didn't close immediately when a curfew was declared. What a gas.

But that's not the end, because there are agitators, quiet types, with *kaffiyehs* over their mouths—as if their mouth was, you know, eyes or something—and with the eyes down, peeking you know, from the corners, to see if someone is, you know, going to open a store on his own, or too fast. And then they make a sign like that with their head and some other guy who sees him signals to someone else, who calls up the store that opened and tells him Look, if you give in to those Jewdogs we'll bash your face in or burn down your store. So there they are, caught between one fear and another, afraid to close when they're open and afraid to open when they're closed, they open and close, close and open. Poor suckers. You'd think they'd be pretty pissed off by now. Us, just from the walking around and around here like we do, we're ready to drop. 'Cause after a couple of days the fear disappears. Evaporates, sort of, and what takes its place is just being sick and tired of it all and feeling that you've had an overdose of the whole thing. Anyway, all that stuff about the eye signals that their agitators and spies pass from one to the other, we heard it from that little Persian, who was a Shinbetnik or something like that, anyway he walked around there in civilian clothes and when he wasn't around we called him "Hundred Grams" 'cause Arnon Dubinski, our religious guy, swore that he'd seen him, that Shinbetnik, helping his father sell sunflower seeds in a store on Ben Yehuda Street. This Persian was dark and he could scare the Arabs even worse than the BPs. Once or twice we saw him beat up an agitator caught after a chase or a storeowner who refused to talk after a Molotov cocktail was thrown—and it was really frightening. There was that guy from the Christian souvenir store, who was twice as tall as he was and three times as fat, he just grabbed him and let him have it, I don't know how he even reached the guy's head, right hooks one after the other, bam bam bam, with amazing strength, until the poor guy's lips and nose and eyes all, you know, exploded with blood. Everyone there saw it but no one had the guts to move. When he was done, and the storeowner collapsed like a, you know, garbage bag on the sidewalk, that little Persian took off his shirt, despite the cold and the drizzle and we saw that his dark, muscular body was all sweated up, and he turned and looked at us like nothing had happened and smiled like a bastard, really cute, with all his teeth sparkling like a pop star, and it made your blood really freeze for a second. I swear. Geez, so little and so scary. Anyway, that Hundred Grams explained to us how the Shinbetniks know like that to read the eyes of the PLO and know how to see where they're sending their glances and signals—and that's how they know who they are and catch them in their houses or on the roofs or on the other side of the street.

Anyway, when that whole business of opening stores and closing stores was done—I really never understood why we needed to do all that. What do I care if they close their stores all day, every day? Do I suffer? They're the ones who suffer. So what if they want to keep everyone out of the kasbah and block the way with boulders and burning tires? So we won't go in. That's what I think, anyway. What do I care? But I'm just a little guy and don't understand much—so when the whole thing with the stores on the main street and in the market is over, we start up again with our patrol. And by then there's action: all of a sudden blocks start coming down on you from the roofs. Boom boom boom. We'd already learned to be careful. Suddenly, just around a bend in the road, you see a few of their guys standing with murder in their eyes, a hundred-fifty meters from us, with iron bars, pipes—inch-and-a-half ones, or so Dov says, he knows those things from the kibbutz—and wave them around to keep you from getting too close. Sometimes it turns into a real fight, and then the radio begins working, like, say, CO from Patrol Nine, trouble at Sheikh Abbas Alley and Hassan Street. Request clearance to fire gas. Roger. Then it gets going, stones, rubber bullets, tear gas, curses. It's become pretty routine, because after all they know they can play on our nerves for a long time before we get permission to shoot live ammo at them. 'Cause the gas canisters, for them, are nothing. One of those falls on them and they just, you know, catch it and throw it into a bucket of water and that's it. But when you have to lug them around they always leak and burn your mouth and eyes and you don't even have onions, like they do, to rub on and stop the pain. The rubber bullets are the same, hurts them a little and then they're fine. We thought that the clubs would scare them. Bull! They get hit and swell up—and then they turn into local heroes. Everyone respects them. You see how they show the black-and-blue marks, under their shirts, to anyone who asks and how those idiot American reporters and photographers take their pictures, click click click. Or suddenly, at the end of the street, there's one of those roadblocks, a pile of rocks and crates or auto parts from some junkyard or garbage cans. Get over here, Glick, our kibbutznik corporal says, Grab me two-three locals to take this roadblock apart. So Dov calls to Dubinski and the two of them go and come back with, say, some old guy with a limp and another, real elegant, in a suit and tie who they took out of a Mercedes that passed by and another young guy shaking with fear, groveling—and they start taking it down. As for me, the truth is that for me it's, like, a little, what can I say, at first it made me feel a little, you know, squirmy, giving people orders, screaming at them, humiliating them. At first, I would even, you know, wince. Don't know why. Truth is, I don't know how I would react if someone did that to me. And since I don't have an answer, and since the whole thing gets on my case, I just swallow and keep quiet. Don't think about it. Don't let it into my head. So they don't see it. Not to disgrace myself. Hey, you need to ignore it. It's like a war. And what can I do? What can I do? There're those looks of silent hatred that you pass over, just take them right and left, and the lips you see moving wordlessly, when you go by, that used to sort of make my stomach knot up, really. You know, not hurting from fear. I'm not all that scared. And not nauseous, either. I'm not like that Ronny kid. I don't, you know, faint from blood like my dad, the doctor, when he was a kid. It knots up and hurts a little from the awful feeling. Don't know exactly what about. 'Cause I know that we aren't scum and they aren't angels, you know, and I understand that there's situations when it seems sort of absurd, but you have no choice. But after a while, you know, you get used to it and your stomach doesn't knot up and, you know, hurt, like at the beginning, years ago. What, when did we come to this damn city? It seems like forever. Okay. What, it's not easy, when people you don't even know hate you like that, and if they could they would knife you in the stomach or in the heart, and as far as they're concerned, they're sure that they're right: We got another dangerous Zionist soldier. *Allahu akbar!*

Anyway, when that business is over—or on a quiet day, which is a rainy or windy day—we finish a circuit, and if we don't, say, have to get PLO slogans cleaned off the walls, then the commander says on the radio that we finished and then he gets a reply that in an hour, ten or eleven o'clock, there'll be a meal at one of the lookouts. That's usually on a roof somewhere or something like that. Then one of those big trucks comes and brings bread and jelly and tea that went cold hours ago and tomatoes and cheese, and sometimes hard-boiled eggs, and we all sit and eat and smoke cigarettes, which are a rare commodity ever since the damn strike at the cigarette factory. And then we go on with the patrol. Sometimes they call us to help the Shinbetniks arrest someone, or to guard the opening to some dark hole in the kasbah and they go in and we hear voices and smacks like that from there, and women wailing, stuff like that. And sometimes we chase someone through the alleys or up on the roofs, and on the way up we crash from the light into their dark houses and we see the fear in the eyes of the little girls, and me, sometimes my stomach turns. But what can I do? I can't control it. Because, really, what do I care? Just like when one of them cries, my stomach starts giving me trouble. Their crying, sometimes, it's like some kind of, you know, electric drill. Penetrating. Kind of grating. Annoying. Full of pain and malice. And then I remind myself of my motto, you know, that, hey, the most important thing is to stay normal in all this mess. Just stay normal. I don't know if I can explain it. Their pain and the hatred and the malice and all that bull, they make it all into some sort of religion, hell if I know, something glorious, say. Something worth suffering anything for. As if they're saying, egging us on, like, Go on, hit us, hit us. Humiliate us, push us, anything, whatever you want— anything for the holy cause. But when they cry, the s.o.b.'s, what can I tell you, inside, doesn't matter how I try not to, it cuts me. I don't know how to put it in words. Maybe because I feel like they hate us more, because on account of those beatings they can't hold back the tears. They cry right there in front of us, cry because they can't bite their lips to keep from crying in front of us. Honor is important for them, so they cry. This annoying wail. Hateful, drilling crying. Screw them all.

Okay. Sometimes we cry too. Here, Danny Peretz who got hit in the neck by a broken shingle from one of the roofs and tried to find out who threw it—lucky that he didn't find out. He was crazy mad and if he'd have seen anyone up there, doesn't matter who, he would have shot him. I know Danny. Lucky that all the scum had hidden fast and you could only hear them laughing, that jeering, taunting laughter—and he didn't know what to do about it, so he just started crying and cursing. Or that corporal from Company B, with the thick glasses, who looked like he was at least thirty years old. His friends, the other corporals from B, started making fun of him one night at the camp, so that all the soldiers could hear: You coward, you Fatahist, left-wing trash, go, go join your PLO. Let's see you go to them now. You know they'll tear your heart out there. All sorts of things like that. He even tried to argue with them, really tried, you know, to go at them, but you know what it's like when you get it from all sides, shouting, refusing to hear and not even letting you get a word in edgewise. So in the end—we stood by the window, on the way back from the canteen, and they didn't notice that there was anyone listening, you know—in the end, you know what, he just went quiet and bent over like that and his buddies kept screaming at him and I saw, you know, tears running down his cheeks.

At night, too, sometimes, you wake up sort of all of a sudden with a kind of cry, into that kind of heavy smell of stagnant, humid air, into that darkness, into the silence with those abrupt snores and the rustlings. And then you realize that someone, you don't know who, is crying under his blanket without feeling it. Don't know why. Maybe I cry like that too in my sleep. Sort of choked back. I don't know. But when someone else cries next to me, and it doesn't matter if it's one of them or one of us, then I tense up inside again. What can I do? No one knows it. And I, you know, I start missing something. Don't know myself who or what. I can't control it. What can I do? I have to get over it, dammit, you know, may she rest in peace, I would tell myself.

TAKING LIBERTIES

THE LITHUANIAN EXODUS FROM THE SOVIET ARMY

LIUDVIKA VILDZIUNAITE-POCIUNIENE

Liudvika Vildziunaite-Pociuniene served as Information Officer for the Temporary Commission on the Return of Lithuanian Citizens Serving in the Armed Forces of the USSR. This commission was established by the Lithuanian Parliament to investigate and evaluate the status of Lithuanians in the Soviet Army; it functioned over the period March 20–June 1, 1990. In her capacity as Information Officer, Ms. Vildziunaite-Pociuniene interviewed a large number of Lithuanian soldiers who deserted from the Soviet Army in the spring of 1990.

Subsequently the commission was dissolved, and its responsibilities were turned over to the Lithuanian Department of Defense. Although Lithuania does not command its own army, the Department of Defense oversees a defense force similar to the National Guard, which is still in an embryonic stage.

Ms. Vildziunaite-Pociuniene lives in Vilnius with her husband and three children.

*O*n *March 11, 1990, Lithuania unilaterally declared its independence from the Soviet Union. Within days of this declaration, a mass desertion from the Soviet Army occurred as approximately 1,000 Lithuanian soldiers fled, returning to Lithuania. Thirty-eight of these soldiers were given temporary shelter by the Lithuanian Parliament in an empty ward of a psychiatric hospital in Kaunas, Lithuania. They were also under the protection of the Lithuanian Red Cross. On March 27, in the early morning hours, Soviet paratroopers stormed the hospital and arrested twenty-one of these soldiers. This article is based on interviews conducted with several Lithuanian soldiers, including some of those involved in the early morning roundup in Kaunas.*

"If you have wound up in the army, then the worst that could happen has happened," said my brother in 1985, just before leaving to serve a mandatory two years in the Soviet Army. Many months of anxious waiting followed. Consoling those of us back home, and maybe himself as well, he wrote playful, ironic letters with little drawings, poking fun at the confusion, stupidity, and ideological idiocy of it all, joking that it was his stomach that was feeling the most homesick. Meanwhile he was locked up three times in a solitary cell, where beating was the norm and food was often denied. His serious run-ins with bullies while trying to protect some of the weaker soldiers were no laughing matter. It was only six months after he returned, and clearly not in front of our mother, that he told us he had also spent time in a special torture cell, where standing up was impossible because of the low ceiling, as was sitting down, because of the ice-cold water up to his knees.*

---

*Cells of this type are still prevalent in the Soviet Army.

But it was not this that was most difficult for him. It was the struggle against his own dehumanization, against his increasing anger at the world, while his patience was wearing thin in a psychologically brutal atmosphere that evokes a "survival of the fittest" syndrome, encouraging the stronger soldiers to oppress the weaker ones. It is a rare person indeed who is able to withstand the system, to remain true to his values. I could barely drag even a few sentences about their military service out of any of my brothers.

You won't hear much more from others, either. I never met a Lithuanian who could speak easily about his experiences in the army. It's an advantage to be older and physically strong, but eighteen-year-old boys in slightly poorer health are often turned into invalids or are psychologically damaged by this "school of machismo." This is a significant problem, because sickly men are drafted into the Soviet Army despite their health. Moreover, many young men who return from the army become withdrawn and lose interest in their studies and often turn to drinking. Even those who are able to come to terms with their negative experience, who do not give in to this process of dehumanization, do not like to speak about it.

With the advent of *glasnost*, the dark, nonceremonial side of army life as well as the military brutality, mildly termed "unsanctioned activity," gradually began to be discussed publicly in newspapers and on television. Those who until then had said that their term of military service had passed normally could now be seen nodding their heads in agreement, as if to say, "Yes, that happened to me, too . . . They burned the soles of my feet, beat me with chairs and belt buckles, took away my new uniform, stole my money and parcels from home, woke me up in the middle of the night and forced me to sing . . . " Victims of rape would remain silent. How could you talk about that?

However, let the words of the tortured and humiliated, who fled the ranks of the Soviet Army a good while before Lithuania reestablished its independence, speak for themselves.

Sigitas:

"Upon arrival at my company, I came face to face with *dedovshchina* [the pecking order by which second-year or senior soldiers haze new arrivals]. The senior soldiers would douse sleeping recruits with water, burn their feet, and force them to work nonstop during working hours in the army factory without a minute's rest. They jeered and beat us for the most insignificant reasons. They took turns watching us work, while the rest of them went into town or sat around.

"There was constant drinking in the unit, followed by a ritual of breaking chairs . . . The sergeants didn't defend us. They ridiculed us, too.

"Once when I was sick and went to the infirmary, it turned out that I had a high fever. Theoretically I was to be granted three days off, but the senior soldiers denied me this right.

"Another day there was a giant drinking fest in the company. The senior lieutenant wasn't around; neither were the other officers. The senior soldiers had us all fall out and then asked, "Who's not going to scrub the floor?" Seven soldiers took two steps forward. Then the senior soldiers, who were drunk, broke apart a chair, took pieces of it in hand, led those seven into the bathroom, and proceeded to beat them for about fifteen minutes. Around that time an inebriated warrant officer came by, and everyone walked away as though nothing had happened. Then one of the drunks came up to me and forced me to clean up.

"This sort of thing was repeated daily. Unable to bear it any more, I fled."

Vytenis:

"That night two Azerbaijanis and I were assigned cleaning duty.* The duty officer assigned the areas that we were responsible for cleaning. When I finished mine, one of the others came up to me and said, 'Now you'll clean my area,' namely, the Lenin Room [a large room], the hallway, and the stairs. I refused. The second one came up to me and said, 'If you don't clean this area, then you'll have to do mine as well.' A fight ensued between us in the Lenin Room. Another soldier showed up and, seeing that I was fighting, took a chair and smashed it over my head from behind. I fell down, and the next thing I remember I was washing up in the bathroom. Other Azerbaijanis in the unit woke up and beat me so severely that I don't remember what happened next. I only recall that sometime later the major on duty picked me up off the floor and took me to the battalion office to explain myself. I was interned in the infirmary until morning. Then I was taken to the hospital for three days.

"When the commanders learned that my mother was on her way to see me, they took me back to the unit in my pajamas. When my mother arrived, we were received in the regiment commander's office, where he and a couple of colonels apologized to us for the incident. After she left, I was assigned kitchen duty—slicing bread in the cafeteria for four months."

This young man's unpleasant odyssey did not end there. One day the keys to the bakery were taken from him and an attempt was made to return him to his previous job. He persuaded his superiors to transfer him instead to the army firefighting unit. Six months later he was faced with a similar series of bureaucratic foul-ups, and he finally fled.

---

*Azerbaijani—a person from Azerbaijan.

Romualdas:

"All the young recruits were pushed around by the senior soldiers: 'Do this, bring me that.' Because I didn't listen, I was hit more than a few times. One winter evening I came back from work and started changing my clothes in the laundry room. For a while I was alone; then P. came in and said, 'Go into the Lenin Room, V. is asking for you.' Four men from our company were there. V. said to me, 'You're going to get it good.' I stood there, uncomprehending, when suddenly he stepped forward and began to beat me. I tried to resist, but he stunned me with blows to my head and face. I felt blood gush from my nose and sat down on a chair. And, urged on by the others, he continued to hit me. They were all drunk and smelled of alcohol. I lost consciousness as everything went dark before me. Afterward P. said to me, 'Go wherever you want, just be sure no one sees you and no one knows what happened. If anyone finds out, you'll be very sorry. If you tell—I'll kill you.'

"Somehow I made it to the infirmary. A nurse took me in and called the doctor and the senior lieutenant. The doctor gave me an injection and called an ambulance, which took me to the hospital. The doctors there said my nose and cheekbone had been broken and diagnosed a concussion. I had chills the entire time. Afraid that they really would kill me, I told the captain that civilian strangers had beaten me up on my way home from work.

"After New Year's, P. and V. came to the hospital to threaten me with physical harm if I said anything. I realized that going back to my company would mean certain death. That's why, when my mother came, I decided to go back home."

It is not surprising that tortured soldiers rarely turn to their officers for help, because there is little hope of getting it. If officers do decide to intervene, by the time they do the victim has usually been victimized again. (See inset.)

In 1989 a law was passed in Lithuania that allowed draftees who had already entered college to complete their studies and additionally exempted them from the mandatory two-year period of service in the Soviet Army.

In the same year a poll was taken of approximately 2,000 Lithuanian college students who had already served one year in the Soviet Army at the time the law was passed and who were then demobilized and allowed to return to college. Results from that survey show that, on average, only one soldier in fifty had turned to his superior officers for help. The majority said that asking for help usually did not improve the situation, but often aggravated it. Some other results of this poll:

— 95% witnessed beating of first-year recruits by second-year soldiers.
— 94% witnessed sergeants beating soldiers.
— 42% saw officers and warrant officers beating soldiers.
— 99% said that serious injuries had been inflicted on men in their units.
— One in thirty had themselves been seriously injured.
— Not everyone was able to withstand the hazing and humiliation. One in two surveyed said they were aware of at least one suicide in their unit, and sometimes as many as seven or more, in one year of service.
— 80% of those surveyed said they were aware of desertions for all of the above-mentioned reasons.
— One in three witnessed soldiers going mad.
— One in four witnessed rape.

There are several reasons for this continued abuse in the Soviet Army: Officers have a vested interest in covering up; physically weak recruits are assigned to the same work battalions as recruits convicted of minor offenses (e.g., brutality and theft); regional, cultural, and religious differences, already a major source of friction in an army composed of young men from over 100 distinct ethnic groups, are exacerbated by the hostile surroundings; and recruits are usually stationed far from their homes, away from family. If any of these circumstances were improved, it is likely that this staggering incidence of violence would be reduced.

But in the Soviet Army a person is not treated as a person—recruits are forced to forfeit their human rights and dignity.

Jurgis:

"The soldier who stole my watch dragged me into the bathroom and explained that here the law of the jungle reigns supreme. He argued that he took from me, and that I in my own time would take from someone else. If I lodged a complaint, things would only get worse.

"I wound up with a dirty, dangerous job in an army factory. I worked as a welder, although I had no training in this field.* I worked 13 to 15 hours a day. Since I am flat-footed, my feet hurt from so many hours of prolonged standing, and my eyes hurt from the welding. My eyesight, which was poor to begin with, got progressively worse. At the factory you had to fulfill a quota, and if you didn't keep pace, or if you took a minute's rest, they would immediately begin to hit you in the legs, the head, and elsewhere where bruises wouldn't be seen. When they kicked my already aching feet, I could barely stand up."

This story is more reminiscent of the experiences of someone deported to a Siberian labor camp than of a young soldier in the late twentieth century. In fact, to this day many Lithuanians endure their service in the Soviet Army as a term in exile. I have seen letters written home by soldiers signed with one word: Deportee.

---

*Apparently, this young man is not alone. The use of soldiers as workers in positions for which they have little or no background training is one of the reasons for a high incidence of accidents in the Soviet Army.

The Soviet Army has always been foreign to Lithuanians. Perhaps it is easier to understand if one imagines being the grandson of a veteran who fought in two wars of independence. Then imagine being forced to serve in the very army against which your grandfather had victoriously fought for independence. It's probably the same feeling that motivated Lithuanian youth to go into the forests in the first years after World War II.* At that time resistance to mobilization in the Soviet Army was particularly strong. Youths joined bands of partisans, whose core groups consisted of former Lithuanian Army soldiers. During the following ten years of partisan warfare approximately 60,000 Lithuanian men were killed—a figure equal to the regular Lithuanian Army and the "Siauliai" movement combined.** When the armed resistance was broken at the end of 1952, Lithuanian youths, under threat of repression, were forced to enter the Soviet Army. It was a rare man who went into hiding, although there were some who did so. Others, protesting the draft, refused to take the military oath of allegiance. These youths faced a martyr's fate: physical and verbal abuse, violence, and life-threatening circumstances.

Concealing their resentment, the majority of young Lithuanian men entered the Soviet Army until 1990, although a rising tide of draft opposition was apparent as early as the fall of 1989. Lithuania's declaration of independence on March 11, 1990, lent added impetus to draft opposition. Nonetheless, even if Lithuania had not

---

* Translator's note: This is a reference to the partisan, or armed resistance, movement that was organized in Lithuania following World War II.

** Translator's note: The Siauliai movement was an organization founded in the city of Siauliai that pressed for Lithuanian independence, both politically and by means of a militia. In light of recent political developments in Lithuania, this group has recently been reactivated.

reestablished its independence, the 1990 spring boycott of the Soviet military draft would have been massive. Current conscription figures indicate that only one fifth of those called up from Lithuania entered the Soviet Army, and the majority of them were Russian or Polish by ethnicity. The others were mainly youths from rural villages who reported under threat of arrest or believed the false promises of military commissariat personnel.

After March 11, Lithuanians began to desert their military units in substantial numbers. Close to a thousand such soldiers registered with the Temporary Commission on the Return of Lithuanian Citizens Serving in the Armed Forces of the USSR. The soldiers left not only because they were beaten and humiliated: Everyone—Russian, Uzbek, Ukrainian—suffers from *dedovshchina* and the dehumanizing process. More often they left because of their Lithuanian nationality. Threats such as "You'll never leave here alive" were openly made toward Lithuanians. In many places Lithuanians were no longer allowed near weapons and were denied furloughs. The Soviet military press has been vicious toward Lithuania because of Lithuania's desire for independence.

But most important, Lithuanian soldiers went home because Lithuania was now free and they were needed in their homeland, and because serving in the occupying nation's army was considered shameful. These words have been repeated by many in their testimonies as to why they left the army.

Caught up in the moment, these boys did not think things through well enough to realize that Lithuania, experiencing its first days of independence, did not have the power to protect them from violent roundups and kidnappings by Soviet military personnel. Perhaps it didn't dawn on them that they would have to go into hiding for a long time.

The Lithuanian government tried to shelter them in the

city of Kaunas under the flag of the Lithuanian Red Cross. Thirty-eight young men who chose this protection were examined by hospital physicians and offered help in recovering from their traumatic experiences. On the night of March 26–27 the medical staff on duty requested that the journalists there leave the hospital premises so that the youths could get some rest. Therefore, the ward was left without even that, albeit noisy and tenuous, "insurance policy." Perhaps it was no coincidence that that very night was chosen for an attack on the hospital by Soviet paratroopers. Saulius Budinas and Kestutis Krasauskas, each of whom had only a few months of military service left, describe what happened to them and the other soldiers that night.

Saulius:

"At about three o'clock in the morning two doctors on duty woke us and said that several military vehicles were outside the hospital, most likely there to round us up. Not fully awake, we didn't believe it at first. After that, everything happened at lightning speed. The outside doors were broken and paratroopers poured in. I had never seen such animal-like behavior and never thought that young men, just like me, could be so brutal. The first thing I heard was cursing. Then they began beating us with the butts of their machine guns, their boots, and their hands. I was hit in the legs with a machine gun and fell down. Then I was kicked a few times, but not too painfully. I escaped further injury, but others weren't so lucky; many sustained serious injuries. Some had broken noses and one suffered a broken rib. Everyone had plenty of bruises on their bodies. They searched us all and confiscated our money, watches, keys, other valuables, and even some better clothing. Those of us who had not managed to dress in time were taken barefoot to the military base at Anadyr, dressed in just our underwear and sweaters. I noticed that the paratroopers had done quite a bit of damage to the hospital—broken doors and windows. As they were taking us out of the building, I saw pools of blood. Some of the paratroopers were pouring buckets of water onto the floor. After that they dragged us to the street with our hands tied. Those who couldn't walk were dragged by their hair. They threw us like logs into two waiting covered trucks; in all, they captured 21 of us. While we were lying in the truck, a major screamed to the soldiers guarding us: 'Kill anyone who moves, on sight!' My emotions in that truck with my hands tied are indescribable. It seemed as if we were being taken to the woods somewhere to be shot. We were a bundle of nerves for having wound up in such a stupid situation."

Kestutis:
"A few managed to escape through the back doors, as planned in case of attack. The door slammed shut in our faces, and since there are no handles on the insides of the doors in a psychiatric hospital, we couldn't open it again. Four of us ran into the bathroom, where we were cornered by the paratroopers, who began beating us. One of us, who was hit extremely hard in the head, later lost consciousness in the truck and then came to. Covered with blood, he tried to get up, but they hit him in the head again. When one of us tried to keep them from tying his hands, they almost killed him by holding a knife to his throat. They also almost broke one soldier's finger trying to get his ring off. We could expect anything from these men, who were acting like rabid animals . . .

"When they brought us out to the hospital yard, we saw a red car pull in. We assumed it was the press—they usually came at night. The car followed the trucks we were in for some time. This gave us some hope that someone would know where they had taken us. While we were being taken away, we really thought they would shoot us."

Saulius:

"We rode for a very long time, three or four hours. The trucks maneuvered a great deal as they drove—pulling into a column of military vehicles, then pulling out again. They brought us to a military airport. (They never told us where we were; all I know is that it was in Lithuania.) We were treated in a more civil manner as we were taken out of the trucks. They untied our hands and led us into the airport building under very heavy guard. They registered us, listing who had run away from where and so forth. Soon thereafter many officers paraded before us, including some generals, declaring that we had committed a criminal offense, having been led astray by the Lithuanian reform movement 'Sajudis' and our 'illegal' goverment. They argued that Lithuania would never leave the Soviet Union. After that we were surrounded by many Russian journalists, but we refused to grant any interviews. They took photographs, but only of those men whose faces weren't bruised. We demanded that they allow us to meet with someone from the Lithuanian government, but they just laughed at us.

"Later, the Baltic regional prosecutor, dressed in a naval officer's uniform, arrived and said that we would not be tried but would be taken to new military units, since we had given ourselves up in good faith! Naturally, we denied that. We said we had been kidnapped and beaten. He answered, 'You shouldn't have resisted.' In fact, none of us had resisted: To have fought three times as many armed paratroopers would have been futile. This entire ceremony lasted about two hours. I had never in my life seen the barrels of so many machine guns drawn on me. They even took us to the bathroom with our hands raised. I almost began to believe that I was a terrible criminal . . ."

Kestutis:

"Two more kidnap victims were brought to the airport—one young boy about sixteen years old, the other about twenty. As it turned out, they were two psychiatric patients who had been kidnapped that same night in Kaunas. They were unable to make themselves understood clearly in Russian. They kept repeating, 'We never served . . . ' The officers retorted, 'So now you will.' They would have flown them out to Anadyr with us, but we insisted that they were not part of our group, so they were left behind . . . Later, as it turns out, things were cleared up and they were returned to the hospital."

Saulius:

"They put us into a large transport plane and flew us out. Where, we were never told. We flew for a very long time. We set down the first time somewhere in the Ural Mountains. Then we spent the night in Yakutsk. And finally we landed in the sunny city of Anadyr. Some of our boys looked funny standing there in the snow without their shoes and in their underwear."

Kestutis:

"After we arrived there was one more moment when we were paralyzed with fear. They were driving us in a bus from the airport. There was snow everywhere. Suddenly we came upon a barbed-wire zone—a prison. We thought that was the end for us, but we drove on by."

Saulius:

"In Anadyr we were received warmly. They dressed, fed, and bathed us right away. They were happy that Lithuanians were being brought in, because Azerbaijanis dominated the base and created a lot of problems for the officers. They all tried to convince us that running away from there was impossible, although that was quite obvious even to an idiot. When there is nothing around for a thousand kilometers and the only form of transportation is an airplane, how could you possibly run away?"

Kestutis Krasauskas and Saulius Budinas served their remaining months of service at the Anadyr base, and both recently returned home. Kestutis is competing for entry into the Department of Sculpture in the Lithuanian Academy of Arts, and Saulius plans to become a lawyer. They were lucky to have been sent to a unit that was tolerable. But not all are so fortunate. For those in poor health it is especially difficult in the arctic region.

The Temporary Commission managed to provide trips to this far corner for some of the recruits' mothers, sisters, and wives. Upon her return from there, Edita Perveneckiene described the place where her husband ended up after his arrest: a harsh climate. Unaccustomed to the low oxygen count, he could hardly breathe; denied warmer clothes, he was hospitalized with colds induced by the chilly, damp winds. The barracks are surrounded by nothing but rocks and coarse grass. Perveneckas' nose was broken during the kidnapping, which is why he is unable to breathe normally; sometimes he almost suffocates. His friend and fellow soldier, Rimas Gudonis, has weak lungs and is constantly tormented by coughing fits. As though that were not enough, they and the other Lithuanian member of their unit are exhausted by constant rounds of night duty. On a good night, they get four hours of sleep. "Let people know that we are dying here," they said.

They are woefully homesick for their country, counting the days and hours until they can return home, like the thousands of other Lithuanian soldiers scattered throughout the vast territory of Siberia, the steppe of Kazakhstan, the swamps of Byelorussia and the Far East. And today, though the major wave of desertions has already passed, some young Lithuanian men still seek asylum, having left their units in the foreign occupying army.

Translated by Ginta Damusis and Ruta Virkutis

X.M.G.

ALY RENWICK

Aly Renwick was born in Galloway, Scotland. When he was fifteen he joined the British Army, signing up for twelve years. He spent the first three years of his service at an apprentice school and the next five years in the Army itself. In 1968 he did a short tour of duty in Northern Ireland. In the same year he managed to buy himself out of the army, choosing to pay a fee rather than serve the remaining four years. He moved to London.

In 1969 Mr. Renwick helped establish the Irish Civil Rights Solidarity Campaign and the Anti-Internment League. In 1974 he was a founding member of the Troops Out Movement, an organization created to lobby for the removal of British troops from Northern Ireland. In 1978 he helped to establish Information on Ireland.

His novel *...last night another soldier...* was published by the Russel Press in 1989.

Mr. Renwick lives in London with his wife.

Niall McCarthy rode his bike round and round with the dwellings facing him and the statue standing proud and fearless in the middle. They said that Cross had the largest square in all of Ireland and possibly Europe as well. Niall didn't know if that was true or not, but it was certainly a grand area for him to put the new bike through its paces. As he passed the face of the statue for the fifth time, he bent back in the saddle and pulled up on the handlebars, smiling delightedly as the front wheel came off the ground for a few seconds.

Jock Dawson looked around as they waited for the order to board the helicopter. The sarge had been telling them that Bessbrook had been a one-horse staging post the last time he had been here. "A muddy field with a few sleepers laid to provide landing and takeoff pads." Now the whole base had been expanded, laid out on a huge concrete slab and surrounded with the usual high corrugated iron walls or "wriggly tin" topped with watchtowers and barbed wire. "The busiest helipad in Western Europe," someone had said, and Jock could believe it as he watched the constant flow of Wessexes, Scouts, Gazelles, and then a solitary Lynx.

"Keep your head down," yelled the corporal, then pointed to the whirling rotors and made a downward motion with his hand as he realized that his voice could not be heard above the surging engine. Jock and his mates raced past him hugging their kits and weapons as they scrambled aboard the helicopter.

Once they were inside, the pilot opened the throttle and the Wessex screamed into the air. Jock twisted his head to view the countryside as the pilot spoke into his mouthpiece: "Take-off completed—on course for X.M.G."

Jock's mind drifted back to the briefing at the barracks in Germany when the commanding officer had told them about their Northern Ireland tour of duty. "Well, chaps, we'll prove if our training is up to it or not—we're set for X.M.G." They had all recognized the jargon for Crossmaglen and felt the tension as they stifled their groans. "The most dangerous place on this earth for a British soldier—and we're going to prove we can go there and do the business. Because if we don't, some of us won't be coming back," the commanding officer continued.

After the officers had left, the sergeants had given their own briefing. "It's the arsehole of the whole bloody world. There's no two sides down there, like in Belfast last time. This time there's only Indians—real mean paddies. There's no innocents down there—they're all in the bloody game. On the surface we have the same rules—yellow card* and that. But if we really want to stay alive, all that goes out the window. Down there we shoot first and ask questions later."

"If you are on wheels, grid line 30 on your map is the line you don't go below, not if you can help it anyway," the sarge had said, indicating a line on the map. "Lots of our lads have been killed down there—Land Rovers, lorries, even armored cars, all blown to bits. Now only special convoys travel by road. Every inch of the route and surrounding area must be checked and then protected before they can pass. So now we travel by helicopter—it's faster and it's bloody safer!"

Jock tried to reconcile those words with the countryside

---

*The yellow card, issued to every British soldier, lays down the guidelines for opening fire.

that flashed past, the little whitewashed buildings with their patchwork of green fields bordered with hedgerows and dotted with clumps of trees and patches of gorse. Could this really be the "bandit country" the commanding officer had talked about, he wondered, as he saw the wooded slopes of Slieve Gullion rising to their left.

As the pilot banked over the town that was to be their home for the next few months, Jock and his mates could see houses and the square. Jock noticed that it looked surprisingly like the town he came from in Scotland. A few people were about and a kid was racing around the square on a bike. Then in the middle was the statue: They'd been told about that. "A stupid paddy screwen a chicken," the sarge had said.

The bike wasn't really new. His dad had got it second-hand, but a bit of cleaning and a dash of paint had done wonders. Anyway, Niall didn't care. It was his bike now and he thought it was great, and he was determined to become expert on it before he had to start school again next week. He'd been so excited that he had gotten up early to try it out, and for a while he'd had the square to himself.

Now the town was springing to life with the local people coming and going, fetching the morning papers and milk and bread, or making an early start to work. As he made his way around the square again he heard the clatter of an incoming helicopter. "The Brits are having a change-around again," he remember his dad saying.

The helicopters had just passed overhead, to disappear behind the corrugated iron and barbed wire of the Brits' fort, when Niall heard the shout. He turned with a triumphant grin toward his best mate, Kevin, who came to meet him with his eyes fixed on the bike.

They met in the shadow cast by the statue as it blocked out the morning sun. The boys talked excitedly as Kevin examined Niall's bike. They took no notice of the statue, which looked on impassively, a figure rising phoenix-like from flames with an inscription in Gaelic and English: "For those who have suffered for their passionate love of Irish Freedom."

Jock and the other squaddies* sprinted from the Wessex, passing the outgoing soldiers who had just finished their four-month tour. The helicopter immediately took off again to make its way back to Bessbrook. The pilot glanced at his watch: twenty seconds to unload and load again. Not bad, he thought. The lesson had been learned. It did not pay to linger in X.M.G. Already some helicopters had been fired at or even mortared, so now the turnover had to be in the least time possible.

Jock and his mates made their way through the cluttered complex to their quarters. On the way they passed the rebuilt Royal Ulster Constabulary post. "The most protected police station in the world," the lieutenant observed. "It's now soundproof, bulletproof, mortarproof, and bombproof. That's why we are here—to protect the R.U.C. and to fly the flag. The anti-British sentiment here is so high, the police wouldn't last five minutes if they were on their own."

As they came to their own hut and ducked to get in through the door, they all saw the message that some wit from the departing unit had left to make them feel at home. "As you slide down the banister of life, you'll remember X.M.G. like a splinter in your arse."

Inside the sparse interior with its rows of bunk beds, the claustrophobic atmosphere hit Jock right away. The only relief from its starkness came from the pornographic pictures that successive army units had kept adding

---

*Squaddy—soldier, member of a squad.

to—until now the hut was decorated with wall-to-wall pinups.

After they had set down their gear, they were taken to the operations room, where they were given a briefing by the captain who was second in command. Behind him on the end wall were maps of the area, with the border between Northern Ireland and Ireland, only a few miles south of them, marked with a heavy line. On the wall to the captain's right were photos of known local IRA operatives, called "players," and on the opposite wall were photos of all the local incidents in which soldiers had been killed. Those were extensive and made a grim impression, as more than thirty soldiers from previous units had died in or around this small town alone.

"The first rule in X.M.G. is to go about with plenty of back-up around," the commanding officer had said. "That is, always go mob-handed," the sarge had added, "so the paddies will know they are in for severe aggro if they start any mucking about."

In the briefing for their first patrol of the town, they were told that three groups of four men each would go out on foot. Corporal Stead would take the middle group and carry out routine personnel checks, known as "P" checks, on anyone in the vicinity of the square. The other two groups would be nearby to give cover.

A boy was practicing on his bike when the four soldiers came round the corner into the square, but like the rest of the people he did not seem to notice the soldiers' presence.

Jock, Orri, and Spider moved slowly around the square, followed by the corporal. They were alert for danger. Across the square they noticed two girls swinging a skipping rope, while between them a procession of their friends dashed in and out, squealing as their hops and jumps carried them clear of the rope's arc. An old man with a dog moved past the shrieking children and quickly disappeared into a house, slamming the door after him. The corporal gestured and muttered something to Orri as the boy on the bike made his next circuit, bringing him close to the soldiers. Orri suddenly leaped into the cycle's path, causing Niall to brake sharply.

Orri grabbed the handlebars and nodded in Stead's direction. "The corporal wants a word with you, sonny."

The boy made to turn the bike in that direction, but Orri maintained his grip on the handlebars. "I'll hold the bike for you," he said.

Niall gripped the bike and made as if to protest, but before he could utter a word Orri leaned forward and snarled into his face, "Move yourself, you stupid paddy, or I'll kick you up the arse."

Niall reluctantly let go of the bike and shuffled toward the corporal. "Name, address, date of birth?" Stead asked, and when Niall answered, the corporal repeated the information into the radio mouthpiece.

The corporal got some information back in reply. "OK, what's the color of the carpet in your front room?" he asked gruffly. "And what's the name of your dad's dog?"

Niall's eyes widened in surprise as he answered the questions. The corporal repeated Niall's answers into the radio. "Good boy," he said, as the radio crackled back to him. "Now have you seen your sister Pat lately? We'd quite like a word with her—just a friendly chat."

As the corporal spoke, a whoop from Orri made them both turn. Niall was horrified to see the soldier racing round the square on his new bike, sometimes bent over the handlebars pedaling furiously, then leaning back in the saddle waving his hands in the air.

After two circuits Orri drew close to Niall and the corporal and yanked on the brakes, bringing the bike shuddering to a halt. He jumped off and dropped the bike on its side onto the asphalt. "There you are, sonny," he said with a grin and, winking at Spider, added, "We're going to liven this godforsaken place up a bit."

Just then, two young men came out of a pub and made off rapidly round a corner. Orri spotted them and, followed by the other soldiers, chased them down a side street. "Stop!" he yelled, leveling his rifle at them. The men stopped and turned, looking apprehensive as the two other soldiers raced up.

"Right, up against the wall, you stupid paddies," Orri snapped. "We'll see what you're carrying."

The men resignedly stood against the wall with arms outstretched and legs apart. Orri handed his gun to Spider and started to search them. First he felt along their arms and legs, then turned to their bodies.

As Orri's hands moved under the second man's shoulders, he suddenly tugged the hairs in the man's armpit through his shirt. The man cursed loudly and dropped his arms, only to be met by a kick from Orri between his still spread legs. The man sank to his knees in agony as Orri bent forward and growled into his ear, "The last lot in here were just boys compared to us. You can tell your mates the men are back in town."

"Run! Run!" Niall shouted, trying to make himself heard over the sound of a helicopter as the Rangers' player scorched down the touchline only to be met with a crunching tackle by an opposition player. Niall grimaced.

He sat with Kevin on the sloping roof of the shelter where the substitute players waited to be called into action. Bellaghy, the rival team, were leading, and Niall and Kevin were excitedly shouting encouragement, hoping the Rangers would equalize.

Years before, the army had annexed part of the Gaelic football field for an extension of the fort, and now the Crossmaglen team, the Rangers, had to play their matches right next to the wriggly tin of the soldiers' encampment.*

---

*Gaelic football is Ireland's national game. The ball is played with both hands and feet.

Another flowing attack from the Crossmaglen team had Bellaghy defending desperately when another helicopter, one of the big ones this time, came especially low over the field, its rotors sending down a current of air over players and spectators alike.

"Don't look up! Pretend they're not there!" someone shouted. But already the game had ground to a halt and the players stood waiting for the helicopter to lift. Trust the Brits to spoil things, thought Niall as the ball was put into play again, just like that nasty one who keeps pinching my bike and riding it round the square.

"I wish they'd leave us alone," said Kevin.

The soldiers laughed when they saw the commotion their Wessex caused as it left the fort to take them to the lookout post. "Stupid paddies playing their barbarian game—why can't they play ordinary football like the rest of us?" Spider said.

The men were flying out to spend the next fortnight on lookout duty at one of the new posts being built right along the border area. On high ground, the construction of wood and breeze blocks, reinforced with sandbags, stood on top of a maze of scaffolding poles. The whole structure was hung with mesh and camouflage nets that gave it a brooding and sinister appearance, with its viewing slits looking out over the green South Armagh countryside.

The soldiers took turns on lookout duty, noting down the comings and goings at the little farms and anything else deemed worthy of notice that the high-powered binoculars revealed.

To relieve the boredom, the squaddies chatted about football or women or any other topic that cropped up. One day they got to talking about nicknames: It started with Sergeant Bold, whose nickname Tubby had a fairly obvious source, to which his beer gut testified.

When the talk got around to the squaddies, Jock and Spider's nicknames were quickly dealt with, the former because he came from Scotland, and the latter because with a surname like Webb what else could he be called?

Orri then told how he had been a skinhead football supporter of his hometown team, Leeds United. He had gotten into trouble for fighting with rival fans, and when he was coming up to court it was suggested to him that the magistrate might take a lenient view if he were to apply to join the army. This he did and duly got off prison but got stuck in the army instead.

He told how at the training depot they were sent for haircuts and how the barbers had just looked bemused at Orri's head, which was still shaved. At the end of a fortnight they had gone on parade for the sergeant major's inspection for the first time. The sergeant major had gone along the ranks and every now and then screamed in a recruit's ear, "Get your 'air cut, you 'orrible little man, you!" Then he had come to the back row where Orri was and stopped at him as if he couldn't believe his eyes. Just below the line of the beret on the back of Orri's head an obscene tattoo could be plainly seen through the fuzz.

The sergeant major had nearly had a fit and screamed at Orri, "Grow your 'air, you 'orrible, 'orrible, 'orrible little man, you." This had caused great amusement not only to the squaddies but also to the other noncommissioned officers, and the soldier had been called 'Orrible from then on, which had later been shortened to Orri.

After they had been at Crossmaglen for six weeks, the commanding officer warned the men to be on their best behavior because a BBC television unit was visiting the town. "They will be talking to some locals and they want to film with us too, so we have to make sure it's our point of view that gets across as much as possible." Patrols into town were suspended for the period, except those that proceeded with the camera crew in tow recording the events.

In the village the crew interviewed several people, including Niall's dad, who made an impromptu speech about the position of the townsfolk. He told how Crossmaglen's natural and historical hinterland was to the south, and how the border was artificial and a logistical headache for the townspeople. "Go on down there a bit," he said, pointing to one of the roads running south, "and you'll see Maureen O'Reilly's shop. Half of it is in the south and half in the north. The borderline runs through the doorway in the center. And out the back of the shop there's Gerry Brady's farm, the border cuts right through the middle of it, too." Local farmers' land had been confiscated for army lookout posts, and border roads that many locals relied on had been blown up and made impassable. He added that the British Army only exacerbated ill feeling in the town by harassing the people with identity checks and taking the land from the Gaelic football pitch to extend the fort.

When the commanding officer was interviewed in his turn, he said that this area was not called "bandit country" for nothing. "The locals have a history of involvement in smuggling and other forms of lawlessness," he said, and added, "The Queen's writ of law and order must rule here as much as in any other part of the United Kingdom."

Corporal Stead was in great demand by the camera crew because he had been put in charge of a little dog called Rats. A former stray, Rats was kept in the fort and passed on from unit to unit. The television crew developed a fixation on the dog and wanted to film it everywhere.

The program was shown two months later, toward the end of the tour. That evening the soldiers settled down in front of the TV set. They were a bit apprehensive about whether the locals' view would come over strong or not.

The program started with a shot of the square, panning

across it. The statue was there, but the commentary did not say what it was. Instead, it said that in Crossmaglen no one wanted to be a friend of the British soldiers except one creature, Rats the dog.

The film showed pictures of Rats, and the commentary told about his coming to join the soldiers and being their friend. In fact, the whole program was about Rats the dog soldier, who was the longest-serving member of the British Army in South Armagh. The interviews with the commanding officer and other army personnel were shown, but no interviews with any locals reached the screen.

The officers were delighted: The locals had not got a look-in, and the British public now had a new animal hero, who supported "our boys," to celebrate.

"Lucky we didn't tell them everything about that bloody dog," said Orri, grinning. "Like how we send him through the gaps in the hedges and walls first to make sure they're not booby-trapped!"

The next morning the sergeant major and the captain were in the operations room when the commanding officer entered.

"That 'erk who was causing trouble with the film chappies—isn't the whole family a bit off?" he asked.

"Yes, sir," the sergeant major replied. "One of theirs is definitely an IRA player, on the run, and McCarthy himself is a regular troublemaker, sir."

The commanding officer smiled coldly. "Well, perhaps we should pay him a visit just to let him know we are keeping an eye on him. You never know—we might just be lucky and pick up his IRA brat too!"

Niall slowly came awake. He had vaguely heard a thudding on the front door, but when the sledgehammer burst the door off its hinges he jerked fully awake.

His feet had barely touched the lino before his bedroom

door was kicked open and a Brit came in. The soldier pointed his rifle at the boy, then indicated to him that he should go downstairs.

In the front room Niall was pushed to join his mother and father, who were being questioned by an officer: "And where is your daughter Pat then?"

"We don't know, and that's the God's own truth," Niall's mother was saying.

"When was the last time you saw her?" continued the officer. But this time there was no reply, just a shaking of the head.

The thuds and bangs from the other rooms indicated that the soldiers were carrying out a thorough search.

"Don't worry, my men are very careful. They won't do any damage," said the officer, noticing the look of concern on the McCarthys' faces.

After they had been held in the room for a tense hour, a soldier showed his face round the door. "All completed now, sir," he said.

The officer turned back toward Niall and his parents. "Terribly sorry to have caused you any inconvenience," he said. He stared at Niall's dad and continued, "But if you go around bad-mouthing the army to the TV people, then you must expect a bit of trouble from time to time."

After the soldiers had gone, the family rushed around to see what damage had been done. The kitchen was wrecked, with units pulled out from the wall and contents of cupboards and drawers all thrown onto the floor. Upstairs the bedrooms were in a similar state, with beds overturned and mattresses slashed.

Back at the fort, Corporal Stead proudly handed over to the intelligence officer the photo of Pat he had found in the McCarthy parents' bedroom. "It looks quite a recent one, sir," he said.

"Well done, we'll get that copied and sent out to every unit to get their files up to date," said the officer.

In their hut after the debriefing, Orri turned to his mates with a look of triumph. "That photo wasn't all we found, lads," he said, thrusting his hand into his pocket. He withdrew his hand and held out some money. "Thirty nicker. I found where the old cow kept her housekeeping. We'll have a piss-up on this when we get back to civilization."

Later, curled up in his bunk, trying to get a spot of shuteye before the next duty call, Jock found it difficult to drift into sleep. He felt a vague unease about this town. It was during the raid that those feelings had come to the fore. Just for a few seconds, as he burst into the bedroom and faced the terrified boy, he had suddenly felt that this could have been his parents' house back home they were raiding, and the thought kept coming back to him. He tried to banish these disturbing notions from his mind and fell into a fitful sleep.

Corporal Stead took up a covering position at the main gate of the fort as the others raced out past him at staggered intervals in different directions, until they were all safely across the road. They took up firing positions themselves until they were joined by the corporal.

In a few days we will be out of this hellhole, thought Jock. He couldn't wait to say goodbye. Although one soldier had been injured jumping from a helicopter, they hadn't lost a man on the tour, and this was their last patrol around the town. No chances were to be taken.

The place was calm, deserted, with no one around anywhere as they walked down the street. They reached the now familiar square and moved cautiously around it. It was so quiet that Spider and Jock jumped when Orri let out a whoop behind them. They turned to see the soldier rushing across the square toward the bike, which was leaning against an end wall.

Orri leaped onto the bicycle and cycled toward the statue, letting fly with a gob of yellow spit as he passed it.

Suddenly he and the bike seemed to split apart in slow motion. Jock heard the sharp crack of the explosion a few seconds later, accompanied by a mist of blood and flesh that sprayed him and the nearest soldiers.

Jock wiped his face with the sleeve of his jacket, trying dazedly to take in what had happened. The corporal broke the silence, detailing most of the soldiers to take covering positions at the edges of the square and notifying the fort by radio. Then with Jock he moved cautiously to the scene of the explosion as another party of soldiers led by the second-in-command hurried from the fort to join them.

The cycle lay a twisted wreck, its rider literally blown apart. The soldiers slowly spread out around the area of the statue and began to pick up the pieces. Jock made his way to a bundle Rats was sniffing and, recognizing the torso and head of his friend in the tangled mesh of flesh and blood, vomited helplessly.

Four days later, Niall McCarthy was playing with his new bike. It wasn't really new, just a secondhand one his big sister Pat had promised him after she and the two men had taken away his other bike. Well, this bike was as good as the other one, it even had new tires, he concluded happily, as he raced it round and round, looking up as the helicopter banked over the square before disappearing behind the corrugated iron surround of the fort.

Jock and Spider were in a somber mood as they made ready to leave, packing their kit and standing waiting for their flight out. Their dash onto the Wessex was given added impetus by the knowledge that this would be their last flight out. Those rushing off it and passing them were here for the next four months.

Well, thought Jock as he settled himself down between Spider and the corporal, he had come and done his stint, had flown the flag. Whether it was worth it or not he didn't really know, or, now that he was leaving, even care.

After lift-off he twisted his head to peer out through the grubby perspex. A last look at X.M.G., he thought, as he saw a boy riding his bike round and round the statue in the center of the square.

Nicaragua in Black and White

Images of a Generation Marked by War

Michael Williamson

Photo by Dale Maharidge

Michael Williamson, a Pulitzer Prize–winning photographer, was born in Washington, D.C. He later moved to California, where he served as a staff writer for the *West County Times*. Since 1978 he has been a staff photographer for the Sacramento *Bee*. His photographic honors include his being named 1989 Photographer of the Year by the San Francisco Bay Area Press Photographers Association; his selection in 1986 as a finalist by the National Press Photographers Association; and his selection in 1982 to receive the Nikon World Understanding Special Recognition Award for national coverage of homelessness and hunger. He has produced award-winning coverage of the war in Nicaragua, the revolution in the Philippines, and the war in El Salvador. Additionally, he covered the crisis in Saudi Arabia and Iraq.

He has coauthored two books with Dale Maharidge, also of the Sacramento *Bee*: the Pulitzer Prize–winning *And Their Children After Them*, and *Journey to Nowhere: The Saga of the New Underclass*. His photographs have been published in *Life, National Geographic, Newsweek, Rolling Stone, Sports Illustrated, Time*, and many other publications.

Mr. Williamson lives in Sacramento, California.

Having already been on assignment in several Central American countries—Belize, Honduras, Guatemala, Panama, and especially El Salvador—I thought I knew what to expect in Nicaragua. Most Central American countries, with the possible exception of Honduras, are green, mountainous, and volcanic; there is a great deal of poverty and large, somewhat dingy, cities.

When I was in El Salvador in 1984, just before leaving for Nicaragua, I talked with other journalists who had spent time in Nicaragua. "You'll hate it," one of them said. "The Sandinistas are Marxists. You go to the airport and they search your bags—it's like a police state. You'll notice the difference right away. These guys are real hardliners. You'll see kids marching in the street practically stonefaced; everything is regimented, and there's military everywhere." I thought, This is going to by very tense. For as tension-filled as El Salvador was, there were also calm times immediately after an offensive when both sides were regrouping and you could count on a brief respite. But this journalist continued, "In Nicaragua you're constantly in a state of fear."

I had been in China in 1983 when things were quite tense there and had noticed that people did not seem to feel comfortable to talk politics on the street, to take me into their homes and show me aspects of their daily life. Society was (and still is) heavily controlled by the government. After hearing this journalist describe Nicaragua, I expected the same kind of conditions there. I thought I would be assigned an official government guide and would see only what they wanted me to see.

Much to my surprise, when I landed in Managua, the capital of Nicaragua, I found that the airport searches, number of guards, and number of armed security personnel was about the same as at other places I've been where there has been a breach of security.

When I failed to feel the tension that I had been led to expect, I felt right away that something was wrong with the journalist's assessment of Nicaragua. It is true that in Augusto César Sandino Airport there is an impersonal little booth where they stamp your passport, and an official looks at you through a little slit rather than dealing with you personally. But that is because he is behind a bulletproof barrier. The airport had been bombed in the past, and security was high.

As I left the airport I still expected to see a somewhat oppressed society. I did see military personnel everywhere, and it was forbidden to photograph certain military installations. Having been to China, however, I know what a classically controlled society feels like, the oppression in the air. I just didn't feel it in Nicaragua.

In fact, I was surprised by the ultimate journalistic freedom that I had to walk around while I was there. Even when we ventured into areas where there had been heavy fighting and approached a roadblock, a Sandinista Army official would say, "Here's the situation: It's really bad up there. There's a lot of fighting and we can't guarantee your safety, but if you want to pass, go right ahead. Good luck."

When we visited villages, especially those in the northern regions of the country where fighting had been particularly heavy, we found that few journalists had been through the area. The Nicaraguans seemed genuinely surprised that we were there and very impressed that we cared.

For instance, I would have curious conversations with people in the outlying areas. They would ask me, You came to our country when you could've gone to Europe or someplace nice? You chose to come *here*? And I'd tell them that yes, I wanted to be here to document what was happening in the country. At that point they would shake their head with a look that suggested they were very impressed but also thought that I was crazy.

One other issue was on my mind when I went to Nicaragua. I was sensitive to the fact that it was my government that was causing a lot of the grief and the war in that country. I wondered if I would be resented, or even if I would be safe. What I discovered when I arrived was that I need not have worried. The Nicaraguans were remarkably sophisticated in their ability to say, You are an American citizen, a journalist who has come here on your own to see what is happening. Your government, we know, is behind the contra war. We make a distinction between the two.

In fact, the Nicaraguan papers constantly printed the results of Harris and Gallup polls showing that most Americans did not favor aiding the contras. I think they were pleased that Americans had some sense of what was going on.

I hadn't known it at the time, but I found out later that the fellow who had told me that I would not like Nicaragua was actually rather well known for his conservative viewpoints. It's just as well that I was not aware of that, because I prepared myself for the worst.

The accompanying photographs are visual impressions from my most recent trip to Nicaragua.

I consider myself a documentary photographer, not an action or war photographer. I like to think in terms of cause and effect. For me, it is important to work symbolically in order to get a photograph that reveals something about what is actually going on. I want my photographs to do more than simply document a situation: Here's a poor child, here's an injured child, here's a rally. I want to reveal the dynamic behind an image.

If there's a pattern to these photographs, it is that I took them when someone looked me in the eye and we connected. To me, the look in their eyes reveals things like tension, fear, anticipation, even curiosity about what I was doing and why I was there with them.

Shortly after I arrived in Managua I attended the annual May Day rally. I took a picture of a formation of girls in uniform. They were between thirteen and seventeen years old and were from a military cadet school. After graduating, they would probably have been involved in the military, although it is unlikely that they would have been frontline fighters.

In this picture, one can see that the girl in front is aware that she's most prominent, and for her it's eyes dead ahead as if she's thinking: "When my commander sees this, he will know that I know the rules. It is to be a soldier, to be in line, and to ignore distractions." And yet some of the other girls are just being girls. The second one in line is looking a little off to the right, the third one is kind of licking her lips and looking at me—she's completely aware that she is being photographed.

I saw one phenomenon a lot in Nicaragua. A teenager with a gun would stand at attention and do his routine because he wanted to show you that he was well trained, that he understood the cause and was dedicated to it. But then you would see teenagers being teenagers, despite the uniform, despite the gun, despite their attempts at acting to give you that hard, mean, just-the-facts, "I'm a tough soldier" look. They would constantly break down and be typical curious teenagers and ask me, "What's this picture for? Where's it going to be published?" It was really a joy to see. I saw less of it, in general, in the areas where there was heavy fighting.

Overall, I noticed two types of young soldiers in Nicaragua: the ones in the cities, whose main jobs were tending to roadblocks, packing gear, and making food packets, and those in the countryside who were actually doing the fighting.

Although many kids in the city had been trained as

soldiers and thought of themselves that way, the fact remains that in the city they could play soccer with their friends, often they were still going to school, there were still some fun things to do in town, there was a little more innocence. Although there was a lot of poverty, plenty of military, and a lot of seriousness in town, the contra war never came to Managua proper.

The soldiers in the countryside were much more tense, much more serious. They had seen comrades injured, had seen death, had been shot at themselves or were missing a limb. There's a different atmosphere when you get out in the countryside where kids have really seen the war.

I learned as I traveled that despite the Sandinistas' massive military capability, they could not place military units in every area where there was contra activity. Instead, in some places they would concentrate their efforts on training civilians to defend themselves by forming a militia.

There were roving Sandinista militia trainers, six or seven of them in an old pickup truck, and they'd drive from village to village. Once there, they would round up the boys between the ages of twelve and twenty who hadn't been conscripted and would sometimes include older men as well.

The trainers would set up targets on a little hillside and run small training sessions to teach civilians to defend themselves. Of course, most of the weapons they had for training were pretty old and beaten up.

I participated in a militia training session in a small village in the region of San Jose de Las Latas, where the fighting was very intense. I took a photograph of a little guy practicing with a gun. The other kids were jealous because everybody wanted to get a chance to fire the gun. They were so poor and had so little military equipment that many times thirty to forty men would have to wait in line for a chance to fire this one gun, and even then they would get only a couple of shots each, because there was a limited amount of ammunition.

They were in a war zone and it was tense and dangerous, but when they got a chance to train with a gun, the men and boys alike thought it was fun and were very competitive.

They asked me if I had ever fired the American version of the semiautomatic machine gun, the M-16, and I said that I had. Then they were insistent that I fire the Soviet-made AK-47 because they wanted to know if there was a difference and which was better. I told them that it did feel different. But they wanted me to pop off a shot, so I did, and they all laughed when I missed the target. They had a good time with it.

Although the Sandinista Army would train civilians, they did not have enough weapons to go around. For instance, when a little village that I was covering was attacked and leveled by a band of twenty or thirty contras, there were only about seven people in the village with any weapons who were capable of responding to the attack. The rest were too busy picking up their children, running and hiding, waking up their husbands to get their guns. Contra attacks were usually surprise attacks in the middle of the night. Dawn was also a common time, when the villagers were sleeping, just getting up, or taking a bath in the creek. In the village I visited, it was a hit-and-run assault. Attacks like this were usually over within minutes.

Next we drove north to Jinotega. In that part of the country there was heavy fighting, and Jinotega was the nearest major city. We went to the large military hospital, where a military physician gave us a tour. It was there that I met and photographed Marben Espinoza.

He had been injured in an ambush. He and a group of

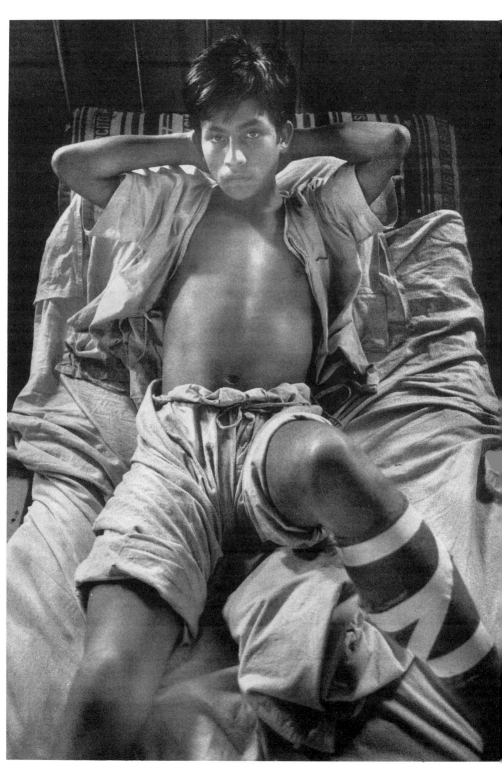

about fifty soldiers were on patrol in the jungle tracking some contras that had attacked a nearby village. The contras knew the army was behind them and had held up and waited for the soldiers to come into their path. When they did, the contras opened fire on them. There were heavy casualties on both sides. Marben had received a nasty leg wound, but it wasn't life-threatening.

I didn't have much opportunity to speak with him. When we were one-on-one with soldiers out in the field, they were usually quite open. I think that some of the hospitalized soldiers were a little afraid about what they could say because their superiors were present.

We decided to go to southern Nicaragua to the region of La Penca to visit a few of the contra camps located along the border with Costa Rica. There was no way to reach them directly through Nicaragua. To get there, we had to fly from Managua to San Jose, Costa Rica, drive for almost six hours in a jeep to the middle of nowhere, park near the Rio San Juan, hike for several miles, meet a contra guide (arranged in advance), and then travel up the river by canoe for an hour.

The area was a contra stronghold, but since there were no real villages there, it was not as if they controlled any major territory. Our base camp had been a contra location for years. It was very small, probably no more than thirty to thirty-five contras, including eight or nine women, but it had several field camps. There was a small one a couple of miles away and another one a couple of miles beyond that, and they kept in contact with each other.

I spent the night in the base camp. When I was trying to sleep I was nervous because planes were flying over and the contras opened fire on everything that flew by. When I talked to the camp commander about it, he said, "Well, none of our planes are due in, so if something flies over, it must be Sandinistas, so we try to shoot it out of the sky."

That struck me as strange because I knew the contras did not have any planes. I asked him what he meant by "one of ours." He said, "Well, we get supplies dropped here." And so, several months before it was common knowledge, I learned that Americans, via an airbase in El Salvador, were dropping supplies to these people illegally. In fact, Eugene Hasenfus, the American mercenary pilot who carried supplies for the contras, had his plane shot down approximately 15 miles from here.

I have to be honest. I was afraid when I was there because they made it clear that the camp could be attacked by the Sandinistas at any time, which was why everything was covered with camouflage. There were Sandinista camps within a couple of miles, so you were constantly vulnerable to aerial or ground attack.

One of my most chilling recollections in Nicaragua involves a conversation that I had with one of the camp commanders.

"Look," I said, "I've photographed the men doing the dishes and I've gone with them on patrol. I've taken pictures of children and their fathers. Do you have any kind of military field hospital here? Maybe I could get photographs of that, maybe photos of a nurse tending to the wounded."

The commander smiled, and several soldiers sitting nearby laughed nervously.

"Oh, we don't have a field hospital at this camp," he said.

"Why?" I asked. "You must suffer casualties."

"In the jungle," he said, "even a moderate wound will kill you because we can't stop gangrene, we can't amputate a leg, we can't sew somebody up. If you get injured to any degree of seriousness, you're going to die. So for us a hospital isn't really needed, because we wouldn't be able to save you if you were badly injured."

Leonzo Dianarto was one of the soldiers I met during my stay in the southern contra camp near La Penca. At the time, he was twelve years old.

I had spotted him the day before and had noticed him

because he was among the youngest contras that I had ever seen. I was fascinated by him. I kept trying to look around for him, and at one point the next day I saw him out of the corner of my eye. I stopped short in the middle of an interview and followed him to his little sentry post between the boats on the river and the area where they stored food. He was just standing there being brave. He had been there, I think, two years. He had come with his father.

He took his job seriously. There was a storage place for food, and he was being very *macho* guarding it. As I mentioned, a lot of these kids would give you the hard stare, the battle-fatigued look, but when you had spent enough time with them they would show their true colors and just become kids again. However, that never happened with Leonzo. He was the real thing, very serious at all times. He was a man with a mission. He was not a boy, but a little man.

Not long after I left Leonzo, the camp commander called together a group of ten soldiers for a strategic planning session. The commander used diagrams and maps as he prepared the fighters to go out on a mission. They had isolated a place where there were some Sandinistas in small numbers, so they were going to go after them.

It was unusual to see contras planning to go after the Sandinista Army. In the northern part of the country they didn't go after the army because they knew they'd be outgunned. Instead, they would go after civilian coffee plantations, factories, and towns. In this case, there wasn't much like that in the area to attack, so they were sort of forced to go one-on-one against the Sandinista troops.

But even at that, neither side really seemed excited about making 20-mile jaunts into the jungle to get into a gun battle. I thought it was strange that we were only a couple of miles away from a major Sandinista camp and the contras had no interest in attacking it. And they had to admit that the Sandinistas probably knew all about them and for whatever reason had not bothered to go in and raid them.

Another strange and rather chilling moment was when another journalist, three contras, and I got into a canoe with a small outboard motor. We went up and down the river to visit several contra camps. When we passed La Penca, a former contra camp that is now a known Sandinista camp, they pointed it out to us.

Wait a minute, I thought, startled. These are contras, we're in a little boat going down the river, and they're telling me that right over there, within 200 to 300 yards, are soldiers from the other side? "We could be blown out of the water, shot on sight," I said, somewhat alarmed.

He said, "Yes, we definitely could be."

I could see the camps in the background. "Is this safe?"

"Oh no, you don't understand," he said. "We're safe because you're here. The Sandinistas are watching us through binoculars and groundscopes. They know that Americans or some kind of westerners are on this boat getting a tour, and they won't fire on us with you in the boat. They have no interest in killing a representative of the western media."

When he was frank with me, I actually felt better, because at least I was aware that we were in an area where the Sandinistas could fire on us. But once he said that we were being used as a shield and would not be fired upon, my feelings came full circle and I felt safe again. It was a very unnerving situation.

We continued buzzing along the river at full speed in this little motorized canoe, with the contras pointing out other sights of interest, when suddenly we hit a log. It made a huge thumping noise, and the impact nearly threw us out of the boat. At first I just grabbed the side of

the boat because I thought it was going out of control. But the contras thought we had been fired on and they hit the deck, so I did too. They scrambled around the boat like scared rabbits, trying to keep low while they got into position. One guy almost jumped out of the boat. They grabbed their weapons and poised them on the edge of the boat and were just about to fire in all directions when the guy in the back called out, "No, no, we hit a log." Everyone got up. We were fine.

One day I was out in Managua shooting some street pictures when a journalist friend of mine, who was based there, told me of an unusual opportunity. A friend of his had just called to say that there was going to be a funeral service at the home of a young man who had been killed in action. They were planning to march his coffin through the streets to the cemetery. "It's going to be somber," he said, "but if you want to document how the war here hits home, you might want to be there."

We drove to a private home in Managua. It was a nice home. Dozens of students, many wearing their school uniforms, were gathered to pay their last respects. Someone took out a military flag, which features a soldier with a gun raised over his head and the words, "Long Live the Revolution." They draped it over the coffin. Several young boys, including his four brothers, lifted the coffin onto their shoulders and marched through the streets. I followed them all the way to the cemetery.

Cevasco Aviles Velasquez, the son of a prominent doctor, and a student in Managua, was the young man in the coffin. He was nineteen years old. He hadn't waited to be called up for military service. Instead, he had felt it was his civic duty to join the Sandinista Army and he did. He had been in the army two months when he was killed.

The funeral was strange for me personally because I was the only photographer, American or otherwise, who was there. It was also very odd to be there because it wasn't a "news" event; it was a private funeral.

My presence was awkward because it was obvious that I was an American. I felt very self-conscious in that this young man had died in a battle with the contras, which my country supported. I didn't really fear retaliation, but I still felt guilty, like a voyeur, taking photographs at a funeral. Something has to be sacred, I thought to myself. Yet I had made eye contact with the parents, I had made eye contact with the students. In a gesturing manner looking down at my camera and up into their eyes, I would dip my chin as I opened my eyes wide, gesturing, Okay? You understand? And their response would usually be to tighten their bottom lip, bob their head up and down very slowly, and blink as if to say, Yes, it's okay. No words were ever exchanged, but I had asked for permission, and they had granted it.

Cevasco Aviles Velasquez was buried in a crypt. They took the crypt lid off to reveal a hole in the ground. There was just enough space to drop the coffin down with ropes. I was within the crowd of young people who were reaching over to touch the coffin. Some cried, said their last good-byes, and dropped flowers into the crypt.

At one moment I found myself on the edge of the crypt looking down, and directly across from me—four feet from me, on the other side, so close that I could just about reach out and tap them on the shoulder—were his four brothers, who had all sort of crowded at the edge of the crypt to look down as the coffin was being lowered. One was crying, one or two of the others were staring blankly, sort of glancing down, one was sobbing.

When I saw those boys crying, I have to admit, the human part of me felt out of place. I felt awkward, but the journalist side of me said, Why am I here? I'm here to document this war and its effects, cause and effect. Symbolically, the four brothers said it all. Anybody could identify with them. They were not in military uniform,

they were just regular kids. It could be any town, anywhere in the world.

I turned off the camera's motor drive, advanced the film manually, very quietly, and raised the camera. I don't even remember focusing. And I snapped just one frame.

I have to say, having shot a million frames, some of which have been very difficult, nothing was as hard to shoot as that frame. I always want to be a human being first and a journalist second. If I had had any less eye contact or less feeling of approval, I could not have done it.

One element that I think added to the power of that image is that the four were all brothers and all close to fighting age themselves. They may have been looking down at their own future.

Several days later, a friend and I were driving near Matagalpa. We had just come back from covering a contra skirmish when I spotted a ferris wheel on the horizon. As we pulled up, I saw that it was a carnival—with old 1950s equipment, from Mexico or someplace, but it was a carnival. Of course, they weren't selling cotton candy or corn dogs, they were selling fruit and vegetables, but there was a carnival atmosphere. Some people had painted faces, and there were games where you could throw the bean bag at milk bottles, etc. It seemed out of place because there was also a little military outpost nearby. There was a fork in the road, with the carnival down one fork and the military outpost down the other.

And this small soldier was standing out in front of the military shack. The soldier may have been a young girl, thirteen or fourteen, maybe twelve, with her hair up, or it could have been a little boy. I could not tell. This soldier was the only one at the post, although I saw a couple of others nearby. They looked as if they were taking a break. One of them appeared to be a sixteen-year-old boy. The

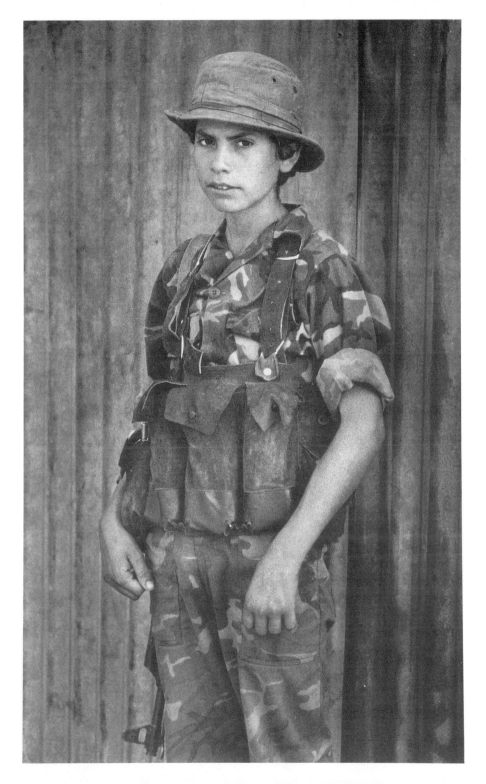

other was a girl who looked about fifteen or sixteen, kind of *macha*, very tough looking. They seemed to be rotating positions.

Meanwhile, we could hear carnival music in the background and the equivalent of, "Step right up and play the beanbags!" There was a lot of incongruity to the scene.

Having traveled with the Sandinistas, I had heard very valid arguments as to why they had to oust the American-backed contras and what their objectives were. When I was with the Sandinistas, their beliefs made perfect sense; I understood their passion, I admired their passion, I respected them. And of course part of their belief was that contras were the enemy, nasty, and not to be liked.

Then a week later I find myself in a contra camp. I break bread with them, I go swimming in the river with them, sleep on their cots, and eat their food. They talk about the friends they've lost, the home that was taken by the Sandinistas, and what the war has done to them. I find them charming and convincing, and I am impressed by their passionate belief in their cause. I come to understand their reasons for doing what they're doing.

So when I return home and someone says, contras—bad, Sandinistas—good, I have to disagree. Is it the other way around, then? No. They both had their moments. They both had their valid points. The strongest opinion I have is that the contras operate more on emotion.

Many of the Sandinista soldiers had originated from a major city, had access to books, and talked about history. Compared to the Sandinista soldiers, more of the contras were illiterate and seemed a little more capable of following orders blindly. Some of them were the children of former National Guardsmen, and they had heard only one side of the story. For them and their fathers, communism was the evil that was going to take over the world and destroy all of man's freedom and independence. They didn't read—there wasn't any reading material at all in the contra camps. It was not that one side was more intelligent than the other, but it seemed that the contras were a little more naive.

As an example, the contra commanders would give speeches in the camps and say, We will win, we will beat the Sandinistas, we will take back our country and march into Managua as heroes. There were two things wrong with that. First, there was no way in a hundred years the contras could ever win. It was impossible. That is just common sense. They didn't have the numbers, they didn't have the weaponry, and especially after the U.S. had officially cut off contra aid, the pipeline of illegal aid was not nearly enough.

Second, after fighting for eight to nine years, the contras had no overwhelming support among the hearts and minds of the people, and no physical territory that they could claim, no village that they controlled. This was despite the fact that one of the largest military powers in the world, the United States, had backed them profusely.

With all due respect to the contras, then, I would have to call them a bit naive. If the contra fighters in those camps actually believed they had a chance at victory, it was wishful thinking.

But by the same token, because of the nature of guerrilla war, had there not been a reduction of the conflict due to the election victory of Violeta Chamorro, the contras could have been a thorn in the side of the Sandinistas forever with even minimal military aid from a country such as the U.S. While the Sandinistas could definitely defeat the contras in general battle and keep them from taking over the country, they could never have beaten them entirely. A very small number of people can create a lot of havoc.

As we discovered in Vietnam, as the Sandinistas and

contras proved, and as we still see in El Salvador, guerrilla wars are 100-year wars. Nonetheless, you still have both sides preaching to their fighting soldiers that, "Victory is just around the corner." That is where I think the naiveté of war is constantly prevalent, in the amazing ability of either side's commanders to convince the troops that victory is close.

I saw troops believing that victory was imminent. Much of the rhetoric in the speeches given to them had less to do with the logistics of war—the number of guns, the fact that we can outshoot them—than with the conviction that morally they were on the right side.

Many of the contras felt that the U.S. was a great and powerful country and would not be backing them if they were not morally correct. For many of them the U.S. stands for freedom, opportunity and democracy, owning one's own home, a car in every garage, a chicken in every pot, Michael Jackson music and Steven Spielberg movies.

For many of the Sandinistas, it was equally cut and dried: The Americans have invaded our country many times. They have raped our land of resources. The Marines have destroyed our villages over the years. History has proven clearly that the Americans are the enemy. So if the Americans are backing the contras, it would stand to reason that it must be bad for Nicaragua.

What I found on both sides was a deep-seated belief that they were right.

A Sound of

Drowning

Pebbles

Bruce Moore-King

Bruce Moore-King was born in Gwanda, Zimbabwe (previously Rhodesia). The son of a prospector, he spent his early years in the bush. He attended boarding school and subsequently entered college to study engineering. He joined the Rhodesian Army, where he served for five years, and then left Rhodesia to live and travel in Europe and Africa. He returned to the newly established nation of Zimbabwe in 1985.

Mr. Moore-King is the author of *White Man, Black War*, published by Penguin, an anti-war novel about his participation in the Rhodesian conflict that led him to reject the values of the society for which he was forced to fight. Several of his articles have been published in the *New York Times*, the *London Times*, and the *Independent*. He is currently working on a novel, *The Cry of the Night Ape*, and simultaneously writing a collection of short stories. The following story is from that collection.

Mr. Moore-King lives in Harare, Zimbabwe, with his wife.

They come upon the naked girls as evening shadows stretch and scattered clouds begin to change from shapeless gray to bright and flaming orange. Birds are starting their evening anthem for the day gone by, the sun is a blinding disk hanging low above the horizon, and soon crickets will begin their chorused tribute to the birth of night.

There are five in the patrol, led by Panos, a square and sturdy Greek boy with almost perfect English. They are five, moving toward a river to fill their water bottles before nightfall. The steady gentle roar of water rushing has been clear for some time, and they have used the same water point* twice before, at about the same time of day on each occasion.

They are almost twenty meters from the densely vegetated bank when they first hear the voices. Panos' hand slices back and down—*Quiet! Take cover!* is as clearly signaled as if bellowed by a parade-ground sergeant major. On their stomachs, they begin to crawl carefully through the bush to the river's edge.

Once they were six, now there are five, they are soldiers from G Company I Rhodesia Regiment, five youths in the seventeenth month of their national service period, a period that has grown from what was a scant twelve weeks when they were still high-voiced children to a now infinite two years as the enemy forces steadily gained control of sprawling miles of bush and mountain, as the operational areas grew like some breed of remorseless amoeba, as the civil war entered its sixth year, and as the

---

*Water point—military term for location where a soldier can replenish his or her water supply.

ZANLA* guerrillas intensified their bitter struggle for dignity. They are in the sweltering northeastern corner of Rhodesia, about fifty miles from the Mozambique border, which lies to their east, and it is across this border that the enemy are swarming. The river to which they are heading, the Mazoe, winds down quickly through the lush citrus estates outside Salisbury,** tumbles blindly on toward the border, is joined by the rushing Nyadiri, then races into the massive Zambezi at a point deep in the Teto province of Mozambique.

Outside Salisbury, white farmers use the Mazoe to irrigate stretching acres of lemon and orange groves. Two hundred miles away, within Mozambique, ZANLA guerrillas use it to supply their training camps, and, somewhere in between, a group of young girls bathe as five tired men move toward them and the day's last warmth begins to fade.

They are five, once they were six, but they have lost a member of the patrol two weeks before, he has been killed, dying, stunned and bewildered, in a blurred chaos of startled shouts and crackling rifle fire and sudden blisters of fountaining dust that lasted less than two minutes. They were left gasping and torn by thorns and rocks, these their only wounds except for the dead boy with staring eyes and a gaping mouth almost as wide as the jagged exit-hole in the back of his sweat-stained T-shirt.

After the sounds of running feet had gone, after they had cleared the immediate area, they had all formed a circle around his corpse, staring back into his aimless gaze, standing mute and silent there, only the rhythm of still-ragged breathing filling the hush from the terrified bush around them, had stood wordless, all, until Panos

---

*ZANLA—Zimbabwe African National Liberation Army.
**Salisbury, Rhodesia, now Harare, Zimbabwe.

had cried: "DOWN! DOWN! Everybody down! NOW!" and they had all hit the ground instantly, a natural ring of protection forming around the dead boy's body. Then Panos had directed them with crisp, tight professional commands: "360 defense! Mike, there! Joe, there! Nick, MAG here! Shane, there!" and they had crawled to their assigned positions, facing outward in a now-defined circle as Panos answered the radio, which had begun to squawk their call-sign desperately. The bush still held its frightened quiet.

They had lain there, not looking back, as Panos dictated a clear and concise contact-report into the handset. His voice did not waver as he detailed the death of Andy Morrison to their base camp twenty miles away.

They had lain there, silent, staring outward until the helicopter with a support squad arrived and rushing men jumped from the clattering machine as it hovered, jumped into swirling, blinding dust, then moved swiftly through the patrol's frozen position, some leaping quickly over the dead boy, dry red dust floating gently down to curtain his dull eyes. A larger circle formed around them and then they were safe. The helicopter swooped back down, nearly to ground level, and they had had to carry the body to it. They pushed Andy in behind the pilot's seat, his feet almost touching the gunner's boots where he sat at the open side of the machine, staring intently out over the slowly moving barrels of his twin Brownings.

They put Andy's pack half under his head and Panos cleared the dead boy's rifle—the magazine was still full, with one round in the breach—and they laid the empty weapon on Andy's body, tucking the muzzle through the wounded chest-webbing, unclasping his belt to lock it again over the rifle's butt. The tip of the muzzle was pressing into the flesh below his chin.

The helicopter clawed eagerly up to the relative safety of its normal height and then back to the Forward Air Field twenty long minutes away, where the body would be decanted into a tin coffin until the next day.

They tracked the enemy until last light, trotting on the clear spoor,* and although the support squad had been dropped in light, carrying only weapons, ammunition, and a single water bottle each, they had had difficulty keeping up with the five men's silent, determined running. They tracked until sunset, and by then the enemy spoor was older than that which they had started on.

By dawn the enemy would have vanished.

They had failed.

The next day the G Company sergeant major would arrive at the Forward Air Field to confirm that the body was that of the soldier detailed on the dog tags. That done, he would sign a receipt for the rifle, ammunition, webbing, and a small plastic bag of personal effects. Then he would authorize a release for the body in the tin coffin to be flown back to Salisbury.

They had failed.

In the following weeks they did not discuss the dead boy. There had been only two awkward moments when, on separate occasions, somene had inadvertently said, in relation to passing conversation, "Do you remember that time Andy . . . " and there was a sudden quiet, a group of individual silences, unembarrassed, but awkward, almost fearful. Then, each time, Panos calmly changed the subject and they all carried on as if nothing had happened.

Now the five soldiers crawl nervously up to the edge of the river, and slowly, gently, move branches and leaves aside. The river is broad, thirty or forty meters wide, but shallow, less than a meter deep.

The bank on which they lie drops sharply into the water

---

* spoor—track or trail.

and is formed of damp clay-soil tightly bound by roots of trees and brush and grass. On the opposite side a strip of clean white sand separates the water's edge from the bush, which is thick and green, dark with growth; there are more trees on that side. Their exposed roots clutch at the edge of the bank, a low wall behind the empty stretch of sand that will be submerged when the river reaches its fill. There are small sandbars pushing up like tiny islands through the swirling water. The river curves away to their left, to the east, and vanishes around a corner heavy with trees and shrubs. A reflection of the falling sun floats just before the elbow of the river's curve, swirling water throwing flashes of gold and bright-white light back up toward them. Looking upstream, the water is clear, absolutely clean, and they can see the sand of the shallow riverbed, can see the outline of occasional gray-black rocks lying beneath its surface.

As they peer, the sounds of quiet evening birds and gently rushing water are punctuated by the distant coughing-grunt of a hippo and the tinkling laughter of the girls bathing on the other side of the river.

The soldiers lie hidden, packs heavy on their backs, rifles held in careful hands.

There are six young girls near the far bank. They jump and run and dive and send whirling sprays into the air, scattered diamonds in the falling light. The evening sun is changing to gold, its reflection deepening in the water to their east.

The dark graceful bodies move easily as they splash and laugh and call, enjoying the exhilaration of sparkling crisp water at the end of a hot summer's day.

The soldiers lie hidden and silent.

The girls swirl and pirouette in their bright exuberance, the firm lines of just-formed breasts accentuating the slimness and natural beauty of youthful waists spreading gently into the beginning curves of femininity. Soft pubic hair holds the glittering sun in myriad droplet reflections that follow the gentle swell and curve of womanhood.

The boys on the bank are no more than a year or two older than the girls playing in the river. They lie silent, breathing carefully, as if onto something delicate and precious and fragile.

The girls shout and call and tease. There is a laughing shriek as one is tripped and ducked by three others; she sits up in the water, spluttering, fist waving cheerful threats as her attackers scramble to a safe distance.

There is a sudden sense of loss within each of the boys, a feeling of unrecognized nostalgia, a sadness, strange and undefined, at the sight of youth and womanhood, the grace and beauty of free and natural expression.

One of the girls steps out of the water onto the stretch of sand and begins telling a story. The others stop still to listen, smiling and giggling as she mimics, using hands and head and body to create the characters she is describing in her tale.

There is a pure knowledge of what should and could have been; blind unthinking, unbidden, the emotion rises, and the boys are completely silent, almost breathless.

The girl finishes her story, and there is a quick clatter of laughing applause. She bows deeply, then sits back down in the water grinning, splashing with her outstretched feet.

The boys lie hidden, there is a sense of loneliness, loneliness and a sad despair that frightens with its strangeness, a fear that grows as each struggles to find its cause, struggles and then, blinded by circumstance, fails, finding only a blank and terrifying unknown. The sun is dropping quickly, and its reflection has vanished from the river; only the tops of the trees hold its final reaching light.

The girls gather at the edge of the bank, kneeling and bending to splash the sand from their bodies. They are still chattering and laughing and suddenly one sprints, squealing, into the river, chased briefly by another, who stops at the water's edge, daring her friend to come back out. It is beginning to get cold.

The boy with the machine gun gazes over the barrel of his weapon, eyes dazed, blinking against a sudden sting of tears; then the fear of shame jerks his being back into the reality of their condition:

They are soldiers.

He looks across at the patrol leader, but the Greek boy has his tightly clasped hands pressed hard against his forehead and his eyes are closed. He looks almost in prayer. The machine gunner realizes that Panos, too, is crying. He moves his gaze slowly from face to face, welcoming this easy direction and concentration of thought that forces his mind to alter its state, to retreat from the edge of frightening darkness that is the unknown, ungrown portion of himself. One boy stares, unblinking, his lower lip white between his teeth; the second has his head down on his folded arms; the third has absently placed an unlit cigarette into his mouth: his face is still, immobile, and the tears on his cheeks are slow and silver in the fading light. The machine gunner looks back to the Greek boy. The patrol leader's eyes open, he drops his hands, looks up and into the machine gunner's steady gaze. There is a brief naked moment, then Panos' whispered hiss slices like a scythe through their silence: "Move out! C'mon! Wrap it up! Let's go! Double file! Chris, take point! Move it!" and reality is once again the stink of their bodies, the weight of the packs sagging into their backs, the gleaming gold cartridges packed so neatly into the black metal magazines, the water bottles still empty at their waists as the quickly dying sun throws its final reaching fingers of shadow and dull orange light.

The group of girls has begun moving away from the river, picking up their simple clothes as they go. Only the girl who had been chased is still in the water, kneeling at the edge of the sand, gazing with interest at a handful of colored, naturally polished pebbles that she has gathered from within the river. She holds them loosely in her hands, bending to rinse them off, shaking her cupped fists in the water, then lifting the smooth and rounded stones curiously to her face, tilting her hands to catch the last rays of sunlight. She looks up and realizes that the others are quietly tiptoeing away. She rises, tosses the pebbles into the river, brushes her hands off against her naked hips, runs up the bank, snatching at her dress as she passes it, calling in sharp amusement after the others, almost alarmed as they begin to disappear down the path. A number of voices call back teasing. She answers tartly and there is a burst of distant laughter.

The soldiers melt smoothly, silently back into the forming darkness. Fear sits, naked, with each of them as they move into the shadows. Only the machine gunner looks back, briefly, as the girls' laughter falls behind them, fading crystals of delicate sound that disappear like forgotten pebbles into the gentle roar of a timeless river.

THE CEMETERY

CHRISTINE H. DABAGUE

Christine H. Dabague was born in Beirut, Lebanon. She graduated from the Sorbonne and became an interpreter and interviewer for Agence France Presse. While there, she was a member of a special video unit that reported on the Israeli seige and occupation of Beirut. She was part of a research team that prepared *Les Fiches du Monde Arabe*, a series of historical reports on the Middle East.

Moving to New York, she studied film at Hunter College. Since that time she has worked on several 35 mm feature films, a documentary, an interactive video, and a music video, as well as on a television series.

She is currently completing a fictional film entitled *Fields: The Anatomy of Mourning*, which she wrote, produced, and directed.

Ms. Dabague lives in New York City.

Early one summer morning a young soldier made his way down the empty, pockmarked street leading to the Moslem cemetery of Raas Al Nabah. He was dusty and unshaven, and his labored steps bore witness to a succession of sleepless nights. The voice of the muezzin calling the faithful to prayer filled the air with its sad, yearning song as he pushed open the creaking metal gate and proceeded slowly down the narrow paths among the white tombstones, oblivious to the sound of sporadic shelling in the distance.

Having reached the end of a row he turned toward a small rectangular stone. Sunlight filtered through the olive and eucalyptus trees and fell onto the stone, revealing a weather-beaten photograph of a very young man. Beneath the portrait, engraved in neat Arab calligraphy, was a name, "Ali," and below that two dates: 1961–1980. Ten years had passed since he had last seen Ali. He had carried his bullet-riddled body home.

They both came from a small village in the south of Lebanon, one perched on a hilltop overlooking the Israeli frontier. Olive and orange groves extended all the way from the edge of the village to the barbed-wire fence where Lebanese and Israeli soliders pitched their tents. The few villagers, who leased and tended the land, had lived in the same mudbrick houses for generations. Like most Shiites* in Lebanon, they possessed very little. Everything—the houses, the olive trees, the oil refinery—belonged to Malik El Din, the absentee landowner. The villagers depended entirely on the olive and orange crops for their sustenance. As landowner, Malik collected half of the harvest.

---

*Shiite: One of two major divisions of Islam, Sunni being the other.

The farmers sold the rest to pay rent for the land and houses. They were left with just enough to get by.

One afternoon Jaafar, then a boy of seven, was sitting by the Hasbany River. The water was cold and clear. The air smelled of thyme and basil, and invisible birds rustled in the trees. He was watching debris float by when he heard footsteps. Pebbles rolled down toward him and someone called: "Hey! You! What are you doing here? This is my spot!"

Jaafar turned and saw a small dark-skinned boy standing on a rock, bare-chested and wet. It wasn't the first time Jaafar had seen him. He recognized him from the village, although they had never talked. The dark boy was a year older and, like all children, kept to his crowd. He came closer and arrogantly asked, "What's your name?"

"I am Jaafar, and who are you?" The older boy looked at him and frowned. Suddenly he beamed a large smile and ran down to Jaafar. "Ali," he answered and crouched next to him on the smooth, white rocks. For a while they watched in silence as schools of small fish tried to swim upstream. All of a sudden Ali bent forward and splashed Jaafar with water, laughing. Jaafar tried to push him in, and they both went tumbling into the rushing stream.

In 1970 the Palestine Liberation Organization began military operations against the state of Israel. From that time on Jaafar's village was repeatedly bombed in retaliation. The villagers would run from their houses and gather in the nearby hills. Jaafar remembered the long nights in the woods. Om* Salah, the old widow, would sit under a tree, her eyes tightly shut. Despite the noise, Jaafar could always hear the regular click of her prayer beads as his mother soothed the terrified children with fruits and stories.

---

* *Om*—an Arabic title of respect, meaning "mother of."

The bombers came sporadically over the next few years until one night in 1974, when the planes kept diving until nothing was left. The ancient olive trees were ablaze, the cattle dead. The wooded hills where the villagers had hidden had also been hit. That night Jaafar lost his entire family. The next morning the small community gathered what little remained and started its exodus.

Om Salah refused to leave. She stood in front of the ruins of her house in her long black dress and watched the villagers assemble. Children cried; old men dragged their tired bodies in silence. Ali and Jaafar walked side by side down the arid, desolate mountain path. Ali's mother carried a couple of pots and pans and her newborn strapped to her waist. His father hauled a rolled mattress on his back. They slowly made their way across the fields toward the sea. They walked for three long days. Finally as they reached the top of a terraced hill they saw the winding coastal road that leads to Beirut. Ali had just turned thirteen.

Jaafar leaned back against the smooth trunk of the eucalyptus tree whose sleepy branches shadowed his friend's grave. The city around him was waking up. He could hear the street filling with the thousand familiar noises of day.

He thought back to their early days in the slums. Although Ali's parents had taken care of him as well as they could, treating him like one of their own, he had missed his family. They lived in a shack by the highway on the outskirts of Ashrafieh, a rich and exclusive Christian neighborhood. The seven children shared one small room with their parents. Refugees from several other destroyed southern villages occupied the rest of the shabby two-story dwelling.

It was a sad but exhilarating time for the two friends, so accustomed to village life. Beirut blossomed in the summer heat. The tall and imposing buildings, the colorful crowds, the movie theaters, and the young girls so arrogant in their revealing western garb—everything fascinated and intimidated them. Jaafar remembered their wonderment as they went from stall to stall through the winding maze of the old Ottoman souks*. They bought ices at the lion-head fountain where Kurds and Bedouins sold their spices: yellow mounds of fragrant cumin and dried coriander from India, lemon grass and large-leafed black tea from China, musk from Burma and cardamom from Iraq.

The two of them would run down the uneven streets past the fish market—where housewives seriously considered their pick, examining and prodding the shimmering scales—and then walk on to the promenade by the sea. Toward sunset they would climb the steep road leading to the shabby old villas of the red-light district. There mysterious shadows beckoned their curious minds and awakened their budding senses.

"We will be rich one day." Ali was sure of it. It was one of those hot and lazy summer evenings. The boys were sitting on the sidewalk by the store discussing the cars they planned to buy. "One day I will have the most expensive car and will live in a beautiful white house in the Ashrafieh hills and . . . "

"Don't you realize that you will never have a car! You'll be lucky if you ever have enough money to get by and feed a family of your own," laughed a young man as he wiped his ruddy hands. Anouar was the son of the neighborhood grocer and sometimes tended his father's store. Ali frowned at him impatiently. "That's what you think! But just you wait and see!" He clenched his fists. Anouar was still laughing at Ali's display of passion when Ali punched him and ran off, Jaafar after him.

---

* *souk*—a traditional Arab market held in arcaded alleys.

The next day Anouar appeared at the family's crowded quarters and invited Ali to come to the small room behind the store for dinner. Ali accepted.

That night Jaafar waited for his friend's return in the dark. The rest of the family were asleep. Their regular breathing helped numb the awkward sadness he felt. He was angry with his friend for leaving him behind. At long last he heard the door slide open and saw Ali tiptoe cautiously round the mattresses toward him, eyes gleaming with excitement. "So, how was dinner?" whispered Jaafar, trying desperately to sound indifferent. Ali barely managed to stifle a laugh. "It was no dinner, you fool! It was a meeting!"

"A what?" Ali looked at him with uncertainty.

"A meeting!" And he added, in a conspiratorial whisper, "A *political* meeting!"

As of that day Ali and Jaafar attended every gathering in the small back room. They already knew some of the people present. In addition to Anouar, Samah the shepherd would come by once in a while. Abou* Hassan, the owner of the gas station, would read the daily paper aloud. He was the only one from the city, and he had been to school. He read about P.L.O. raids against Israel and Israel's bombing of southern Lebanon, the area from which Ali and Jaafar had so recently fled. Anouar's father would sit in his favorite chair and shake his head disapprovingly while preparing the water pipes for the men to smoke.

The boys sat in on the tedious all-night political discussions. They listened as Anouar described the history of Lebanon. In 1943, he said, when the French gave Lebanon its independence and established its current borders, the Lebanese constitution was written. It divided

---

Abou— an Arabic term of respect that means "father of."

political power among the several religious groups in proportion to their number, and so Christians received the greatest share of power. The proportions were fixed in the constitution. By 1970 the Shiites had become the majority of the population, but they still had only a small share of political power. The imbalance was at the root of the current unrest, Anouar explained. He also talked about the need for change and the possibility of revolution. Even the older men treated him with respect. He knew so much!

About that time, a small skinny mutt appeared in the neighborhood. The dog made a terrible mess as he dug in the garbage piled on the street. The children chased him, throwing stones and yelling. Jaafar got into the habit of feeding him, and the dog started to follow the boy everywhere. At night he would curl up on the doorstep outside and wait for Jaafar till morning, jumping up when he appeared. Ali made fun of his friend's new acquaintance and ridiculed his scraggly appearance.

The winter of 1975 was very cold. Every other day universities and workers' unions in the city went on strike. In the small community, Anouar's meetings became an increasingly popular activity.

The men spent hours discussing the deteriorating economic situation, and the boys listened intently. Anouar explained that the economic gap between the religious communities had grown steadily over the past decade. The Christians and upper-class Sunnis had gotten richer while the rest of the Moslems, although the majority of the population, were still at or near the poverty level. Anouar also began to discuss the possibility of armed struggle to overthrow the Conservative government.

Violent confrontations between strikers and police were now daily occurrences. An uneasy hostility slowly settled between different communities, and fear gripped the city.

One late afternoon the two boys went to visit Abou Hassan at his gas station. They were discussing cars as usual when Anouar came running down the highway. He was breathless and pale. As soon as he reached them the terrifying news came gushing out of his trembling lips. A massacre. He'd seen it . . . The Christian militia had circled the square, had stopped a bus in which some unarmed Palestinians . . . They kept shooting . . . they kept shooting . . . Bodies were lying everywhere.

The boys could not go to Ashrafieh anymore. Tensions were running very high, and the Christian stronghold became extremely dangerous. Weapons became common in the neighborhood. Abou Anouar had a couple of automatic rifles stashed in the store. Samah the shepherd carried a gun under his ragged woolen coat.

One night a man they had never seen came to Anouar's meeting. He was older than all those present. His face was weathered and his cheeks sunken. Although he sat quietly in a dim corner of the room, everyone was aware of his imposing presence. Anouar finally introduced him. His name was Abou Samra and he was a Fedayee*. "I have come to discuss the possibility of organizing your group into a neighborhood militia," he said. "I will provide the necessary weapons, and the party will pay you a monthly wage." Although Ali and Jaafar asked to join, Anouar refused to give them weapons. "You are too young," he explained.

A few days later the long-expected civil war broke out. An alliance of Christian factions—the Maronite militia, the Phalangists, and others—battled throughout the city against a rival alliance of Sunni, Socialist, Shiite, and Palestinian factions.

---

*Fedayee: literally, a guerrilla fighter. The term is used primarily by the P.L.O.

The boys would follow the armed men through the deserted streets. They had forgotten about cars. One day Ali approached Abou Samra and asked to see his gun. He handled the automatic rifle, caressing it lovingly. The old fighter watched him and smiled.

"To carry a gun you have to be a man, you have to kill, you have to die without fear. One day . . . " he said softly as he tried to take the weapon from the boy's stubborn hold. Ali stared at him defiantly and pulled away. He cocked the gun, his eyes searching desperately for a target. The dog was lying on the sidewalk by Jaafar. Ali aimed. The small body slumped down on its side. Its fur was torn to shreds, and thick blood quickly pooled on the ground at Jaafar's feet. Ali stood staring. Abou Samra removed the rifle from his now yielding hands.

Jaafar heard a bestial shriek as he lunged for Ali's throat. It was the sound of his own voice. He knocked his friend to the ground, where they fought passionately until Abou Samra and some other men pulled them apart.

Jaafar stopped going to the meetings. He moved out of the family's dwelling, found a job at the bakery, and settled in with the young baker and his wife. Soon after, Ali got into a habit of picking up the family's bread. He would walk into the bakery every morning, his eyes searching the store expectantly. Jaafar avoided him.

As the suffocating heat of summer hung more heavily over the city, the fighting spread and the battles grew more fierce. One night Jaafar was walking down the empty street when he spotted Ali's mother standing in front of Anouar's closed grocery. She stood alone in the dark, banging fiercely on the metal gate. She turned to Jaafar. Recognizing him, she let out a cry and took him by the arms.

"You must know! Where is he?" Jaafar didn't understand the question at first. It finally sank in, and he was

surprised to realize that he still cared about Ali. She had
looked everywhere, the woman said. Ali was nowhere to
be found. Jaafar had not seen him since earlier that day, at
the bakery. He had been with a group of young fighters.

"But he didn't bring me bread today! Who were they?
Was it Anouar?" she said and banged harder on the gate.
Jaafar looked down. "No, not Anouar... I don't
know..." he whispered.

That night Jaafar sat with Ali's family in the dark, all of
them huddled round the small portable radio. The electric
plant had been hit, and they had run out of candles. They
listened as if mesmerized by the commentator's gloomy
voice. The city center was burning. Battles raged in every
alleyway. As the commentator sternly read out the names
of the dead, Ali's mother sat in a corner clutching her
youngest child to her bosom. She kept rocking back and
forth, her eyes fixed on the door.

A week passed with no word of Ali. A cease-fire was
declared. That morning, Jaafar managed to get some bread
and joined Ali's family for breakfast. They were eating
when they heard familiar footsteps running up the stairs.

His clothes were torn and muddy, his face was black
with dirt, his eyes shimmered with excitement, and he
carried a gun. He laughed at his father's angry shouting,
his mother's wailing... How proud Jaafar was to hear
his friend speak! He saw the yearning and resolve and Om
Ali's sad eyes. A few days later he enlisted in the same
militia as his friend.

From that time Jaafar fought side by side with Ali. Their
first battles together were full of excitement and joy. They
laughed as mortars fell, they were happy. Life was never
so beautiful: The hot sun baked their young bodies, the
city was burning, every moment was their last. They were
not poor, they *were* something. They could change the
course of things. They had the power of life and death.

Ali was so eager! He loved the heat of the long sleepless

nights they spent roaming the dark war-torn streets. They went from barricade to barricade through the intricate web of streets in the Old Market, along the demarcation line dividing the city into East and West. The stalls and the bustle, the scent of spices and the chatter of women had disappeared long ago. Night after night Ali and Jaafar waited for their prey, crouched behind the rubble, their hearts beating fast. As cease-fire after cease-fire was broken, the demography of Beirut changed. Three long, violent years went by and the city became divided. The old souks became the permanent frontier between the Christian sector in the East and the Moslem sector in the West.

After three years of civil war, Ali, now seventeen, and Jaafar, sixteen, welcomed the uneasy truce that was finally established. They spent long lazy days on the white sandy beaches and visited the beautifully painted girls in the once forbidden villas by the shore. They met and befriended the old man Saade, who owned the best brothel on the hill. He was fat and pale, and his sunken wet eyes seemed never to see the light of day. He always sat in the dark living room on his moth-eaten red velvet couch, watching lustfully as his customers frolicked. He treated the boys well, and Ali liked his company. Ali and Saade soon started having secret conferences. Jaafar knew the decrepit man to be a smuggler, but Ali never made him privy to their affairs. One day Ali announced that he and Saade had to go away for a while. "On business," he said. Jaafar didn't ask questions as Ali bid him farewell. Weeks passed. Every day Jaafar visited Saade's women, but they knew nothing. Finally one morning, Saade returned alone.

Several months later Jaafar was visiting the old neighborhood. He stood on the sidewalk by the grocery store watching the old men play backgammon. Someone's radio was on, and Om Kalthoum was singing a mournful love ballad. Abou Hassan, who was winning the game, dared anyone to challenge him. They were all laughing when a man walked up and leaned heavily on the peeling wall next to the store. The laughter stopped. Jaafar looked up, and what he saw filled him with horror. The stranger's face was lacerated and swollen. Blood-stained clothes hung from his broken body. His head was shaved. He seemed very old.

"I missed you, friend," said the man in a whisper. Jaafar felt his knees shake as he recognized the voice. He stared incredulously. He could not hear the music anymore, he could not see the littered street and the run-down buildings. Everything had become a blur. Suddenly he felt a surge of savage angry joy.

"It is you! You're alive! You're here! Ali! It's Ali!" he screamed triumphantly. As he embraced his friend, Jaafar noticed that the old men had all stood up in silence. He cringed when he saw the pity in their tired eyes.

Nobody could recognize the bloodied young fighter. Even his mother looked at him with a blank stare when Jaafar first brought him home. And he was never the same. Although he recovered his strength, anger had become the driving force in his life.

When war broke out once more, Ali threw himself into battle with despair, oblivious to danger. He refused to take prisoners. His fellow fighters, Jaafar included, watched with horrified disbelief as he executed wounded men. He never talked of the torture he had suffered and avoided showing his scarred body. He refused to go swimming, shunned the brothels in Zeitouni, and remained alone most of the time. He never told Jaafar what had happened.

At the end of November Ali and Jaafar's unit was assigned to a barricade along the demarcation line. Facing them, just across the street, was a tall building: the stronghold of the Christian militia. It was raining hard and the night was pitch black. Jaafar could not see more than a few feet. The unit was running out of ammunition, and their opponents had the upper hand. They waited anxiously for the next attack. Around midnight the rain finally stopped. "They will attack any minute now," said Jaafar in a whisper.

Ali sat back against the damp sandbags and looked up at his friend, who was peering over the barricade. The sound of crickets filled the air.

"Do you remember the village?" he asked. Jaafar nodded and slid down to his friend's side. Ali's voice floated softly through the eery silence. He described the sloping, sleepy hills, the looming snow-covered mountains, and the distant, hazy blue line of the sea below. He recalled trying to keep up with his mother as she climbed to their small plot of land. They would leave the village at dawn and make their way up the terraced hills. She was young and so beautiful . . . Her long black tresses moved to and fro as she climbed, out of breath. Sometimes she looked back and smiled at his clumsy efforts to keep up. She always knew when to stop, just as he was about to give up. She always had fruit hidden in the large pockets of her long colorful dress. They would squat side by side on the dark, scented earth, by the chestnut tree, and in her whimsical out-of-tune voice she would tell him tales of genies and witches and sultans and thieves. The same stories again and again . . .

Suddenly the sound of gunfire shattered the quiet and all hell broke loose. Jaafar gripped his weapon and looked at his friend. Ali was laughing. He jumped over the sandbags and ran down the middle of the street, laughing.

Jaafar could still hear his beautiful arrogant laughter defying the sounds of war, echoing on and on against the shattered walls of the looming buildings. He picked up the rifle he had laid down on the damp earth and squinted at the sky. The sun was already high. He passed a weary hand over his unshaven face. He was tired, so horribly tired. He looked one last time at the smiling young man in the photograph and pulled himself up heavily. Ten years! Had anything changed?

Checking his watch, he realized he was late. Walking quickly, he made his way down the narrow paths, past the black-clad women tending their graves, back into the sunny street of his broken city.

TIENANMEN
SQUARE
A SOLDIER'S STORY

XIAO YE

Xiao Ye was born in China, the son of an army general. When he was fourteen he joined the People's Liberation Army of China. He served in the army for five years.

Mr. Xiao was in Beijing at the time of the Tienanmen Square demonstrations and the subsequent crushing of the protest by the People's Liberation Army. He witnessed the profound impact these events had on the Chinese people. His time in the army made the clash between citizens and soldiers particularly painful.

"Xiao Ye" is a pseudonym. The author is an exile who currently lives in the United States.

"How could the People's Liberation Army attack us, the citizens of Beijing?"

"Never in the history of China have the Army's tanks been turned against the Chinese people!"

"Our leaders are like fathers, and the soldiers are like uncles to us—how could they betray us?"

These and many other expressions of shock echoed throughout Beijing the morning after the violent suppression of demonstrations for political freedom in Tienanmen Square on June 4, 1989. After fifty days of jubilant protest by students and workers, many of whom had set up squatters' housing in the square, the demonstration had become the focus of international attention and an embarrassment to the Chinese leaders. Whatever the degree of dissent in the square, however, whatever level of anger the Party leaders might have felt toward the demonstrators, no one believed it possible that the Army would open fire on their own.

Days after that very occurrence, I stood watching the troops marching across the now depopulated square. My mind turned back to the early days of the protest.

Even then I had an uneasy premonition of the violence to come. And when I first spoke with my father about the demonstration, that uneasiness grew. As a retired Army general who had devoted his entire life to the Party and the revolution, Father regarded anyone who questioned the Party as a counter-revolutionary. In his view, the students and workers in the square were intent on dismantling everything he and his comrades had striven to create for more than fifty years. He listened with tight-lipped disapproval as I described what was happening at Tienanmen.

I knew his attitudes to be in keeping with those of his generation, a reflection of the resentment harbored toward the demonstrators by the gerontocracy in power. My father could not accept the idea that the protesters might be seeking a new vision for China. For him, the issue was black and white: The demonstrators did not respect those who had sacrificed everything for this same China, for the sake of *these very demonstrators* and their happiness. If they respected all that had been done on their behalf, he reasoned, those rebels would not now be embarrassing the Party. I felt my enthusiasm evaporate in the face of his obvious displeasure.

The days wore on and the demonstration flourished. Many became increasingly hopeful that political change and new political freedoms would come peacefully to China. I continued to visit my father, but we found less and less to say to each other.

One night the lights in the square were turned off. No one knew what to make of it. Tanks and armored personnel carriers rolled into the square. Soldiers began firing on the dissenting citizens of Beijing, some of whom were in their makeshift tents. The soldiers, some fresh from the provinces, many with a wild roving fear, fired into the unarmed crowd and people scattered, tripping in the darkness as they tried to escape. People were shaken and stunned. Their assumptions about the Army's role as protector of the people were shattered as surely as the demonstration was brutally overrun. China was a family at war with itself, and Tienanmen was the dragon biting its own tail. But that circular motion of frustration was the outcome of a process that had other beginnings.

Standing now looking at the square, I thought about the soldiers of Tienanmen. I recognized their uniforms, every button and seam; I knew the shape, weight, and capability of their automatic weapons; many times over I had heard the command that caused them to fire. I, too, had once been a soldier in the People's Liberation Army.

I still remember clearly the morning I said good-bye to my father and set off to join the Army. I was all of fourteen. Father had held a high position in the government but had been criticized during the Cultural Revolution and had been sent to the countryside to do manual labor. For a similar reason, Mother had been sent for re-education to a village more than forty miles away. Father and I were living alone in a small hut on a hill overgrown with weeds.

I walked into the hut, pack on my back, to say good-bye. My father was sitting there on the dilapidated bed with a gloomy look on his face. I felt for the first time that I stood before him as a man. I was going to join the Army, his Army, leaving home as he had done more than thirty years earlier.

It was a great day for me. For my generation, which came of age in the 1970s, to become a soldier in the Army and serve the Party was the noblest ideal. Catching a lift on a truck heading toward the train station, I was filled with the passionate certainty that I had taken the first step on the road to my destiny.

Five nights later I was hundreds of miles away, on Shanxi Road in Nanjing, in a fashionable neighborhood where high officials lived. I stood on the porch of one of my father's old wartime comrades, a general and chief of staff to the commander of the Nanjing military district. Fingering the letter of introduction that my father had written for me, I nervously rang the bell. The guard who answered the door told me that the general and his family were at the theater. I told him the reason for my visit, but he closed the door on me. I sat down beside the door and fell asleep.

I don't know how much time passed before I was jolted awake by a shout. The general and his family had returned home to find someone sitting in the shadows near the door. Thinking I might be an assassin, the general's bodyguard had immediately drawn his gun. Later that night the general apologized and explained that another high official, someone who had been on the wrong side of the political struggle between Chairman Mao and Marshal Lin Biao, had only recently been assassinated in his home.

The general took me with him to military district headquarters a few days later. We walked into the main building, which looked more like a mansion than an office, with its hardwood tables and chairs and comfortable sofas. Another officer arrived with two teenaged boys, also sons of the general's wartime companions. The general had arranged for all three of us to join the Army together.

The general had personally inducted the sons of so many high-level cadres and military officials that they could form an entire company. During the conscription season at the beginning of each year his home was filled with them. The general was a man who valued friendship. In those days there was no better way to prove his friendship than to assist people's children into the Army. Perhaps in the complex web of human relationships it was one of the most important routes to officialdom in China.

The unit I joined was directly attached to the Nanjing military district, and my camp was situated about twenty-five miles southeast of Nanjing. I was introduced to the staff officer, a heavyset man with a kind, avuncular attitude toward his men. He politely asked me what I wanted to do. I said anything at all would be fine: menial duties, cooking, raising pigs. If only I could be a soldier and fight the Russians and the Americans, I said, any amount of misery or fatigue wouldn't matter. He looked both surprised and pleased.

He asked me my age. I lied and said that I was sixteen. He thought for a moment and decided to send me to Company X. That was his old outfit, he told me, and I knew from this assignment that he liked me. He summoned a soldier, who escorted me to the company barracks. I was delighted. I was finally a soldier.

In China to say, "I was a soldier" is like saying, "I can take hardship." Not only is military life tense, but the training is primitive and spartan. Chinese soldiers have a saying, "If you sweat a lot in ordinary times, you bleed less in wartime." The principles of training serve to increase the pressure and hardships that the soldier is able to tolerate. This better equips him for war.

Military life was very strictly regulated. Our clothing, the length of our hair, the way we walked, the respect we showed to senior officers—all were specifically regulated. Everyone got up, trained, ate, and went to bed at the same time. If it was not time for lights out, you could not even touch the side of your bed.

Every morning at 5:00 a.m. we would be awakened by a bugle reveille. I would leap out of bed, throw on my shirt, button it up, pull on my trousers and button them up, and then fasten my belt as I rushed out of the room. If I were fast enough there would be time to pee in the big vat around which a line of men had already formed; otherwise I'd have to hold it in while we did our morning run of four to five miles. Needless to say, that was not easy.

Later I became more experienced. When I heard the wake-up signal I pulled on my shirt, trousers, and hat, hung my battle gear around my neck, and raced out of the barracks, buttoning and straightening my uniform as I ran. That way, I wouldn't be late.

Antitank training was an important part of our military training. In those days, when all we had at our disposal were firebombs, hand grenades, and bazookas, we also had a saying: "A squad should swap their equipment and lives to disable an enemy tank." We practiced different means of getting close enough to a tank—sometimes even running up to it—to be able to blow it up. Our drills included even more primitive practices such as throwing Molotov cocktails or inserting wooden poles in the tread of a tank to stop it.

It was felt that by using these tactics we could sap the enemy's strength and stop his advance. Like everyone else, I resolved to sacrifice my life for this purpose. Diagrams of the Soviet T62 and the American M1 tanks were posted all over the camp, so all of the soldiers were acquainted with their capabilities and firepower.

In 1970, the year I entered the army, a special effort was made to upgrade the fighting capacity of the troops. The military units set up special training groups called "guidance teams." The members were selected from the technical core of each company, who were given intensive training so that they could return to their units and serve as trainers. I was chosen to be on a regimental guidance team.

Our squad instructor was as strong as an ox and swarthy, brainless but knowledgeable about military technology, an old pro. He had fought in the Civil War. His military record was good, but because he was not educated, he was never promoted. He didn't care a whit about the political discussions bandied about the camp, and it didn't seem to matter to him with whom he was fighting. As long as there was fighting and he had a part in it, he was satisfied.

He was very demanding of the men on his team. He would often point out a high hill and order us to use tactics to secure it within a given number of minutes. When we practiced shooting from a prone position, he made us crawl in the hot sun for several hours. If someone got tired and tried to sneak in a little shifting movement, he would give him a swift kick. When he ordered us to charge forward and dive to the ground, he wanted us to dive very fast and continue to slide headlong for a few yards, since that was the only way he could determine our speed. The skin on my knees and elbows would be scraped off, but as he said, the speed with which you can get down is critical on the battlefield, because losing a few seconds could cost your life. He taught us: "To be a good soldier you should stand like a pine tree and sit like a grandfather clock, awe-inspiring and stern." I learned quite a lot about fighting from him.

One of the things I liked least was being taken out of camp to live and train in the open. This type of training began in 1970, when Mao Zedong observed that during the Civil War he himself had never stayed in a military camp. He ordered the Army to train in the wilderness so that we would be tough in time of war.

Thus it happened that every winter all field armies held large-scale maneuvers. Each day we normally marched 20 to 25 miles, sometimes more. Every man had to carry his gun, four hand grenades, more than 100 bullets, a small iron shovel, several pounds of dry rice, and a canteen. In addition we carried a satchel containing a military comforter, a change of uniform, and a pair of rubber-soled shoes. A raincoat that doubled as a tarpaulin was tied to the top of our pack. Taken together, this equipment weighed between 85 and 100 pounds. We also had to take turns carrying the ammunition crates.

These marches involved crossing mountain roads and dirt roads. Sometimes there was no road at all. When crossing mountainous regions we had to use our arms and legs like gorillas, taking a step and then grabbing a tree, or crawling up a cliff.

Hiking at night was particularly dangerous, especially when it was raining in the mountains. All lights were forbidden in order to guard against aerial reconnaissance, so you could only follow the sound of the feet ahead of you and rely on your senses. Slipping and sliding in the mud, I would grit my teeth at every pace, never sure where I might put my foot down.

One night I heard a sloshing sound ahead of me. I

reached out and grabbed at what I could, a foot that had slipped, and I slid after it. The file of men ahead of us had made a turn before a precipice, but the soldier in front of me had not seen it and had kept going straight. Three or four of us fell off the cliff with him into a wet rice paddy.

We usually developed bleeding blisters on our feet after a few days of this kind of hiking. Our feet were a mass of soggy peeling flesh and blood, and the pain was almost unbearable. Empty vehicles followed after us, and anyone who wanted to could get a lift, but very few chose to. We considered the physical challenge a means of tempering ourselves for the sake of the Party. That attitude was encouraged by the political cadres, who walked back and forth among the ranks exhorting us: "This is the point at which the Party is testing you." In that kind of situation, no one wanted to look bad.

After walking for ten hours, my pack and the gun on my shoulder seemed to weigh a thousand pounds. My feet felt as if they had been cast in lead. Every step took great effort. My greatest desire was to lie down and rest, even if it was raining or snowing, even if it meant that I would die. Several times I started to doze off; the man behind me would bump into me and wake me up.

Of course, when we had reached our goal we still could not rest. We had to build fortifications, make camouflage, set up a communications system, and in all respects prepare ourselves to fight a battle. It was exhausting.

Once when a platoon commander was trying to make a telephone call the female operator asked why he was so short of breath. He answered grumpily, "We've just marched more than 30 miles; who wouldn't be short of breath?" Later he was reprimanded because of that one sentence: A revolutionary soldier should not care how much he has endured; he must never complain.

We were also required to devote a lot of time to political studies. Our texts were Mao's writings as well as editorials from the official newspapers. Each company had lessons in basic political terms and information, which we were usually required to memorize. When I joined the army the influence of the Cultural Revolution was still strong, and every evening we lined up under Mao's portrait. The squad leader would speak for us, "reporting to Chairman Mao" what we had done for the sake of the revolution that day, what mistakes we had made, and what we resolved to do tomorrow.

The Army also had a policy of "recalling the suffering of the old society." The political officers often invited a toothless old woman and other peasants from a neighboring village to tell us about life before the revolution. The old woman would wipe away her tears as she spoke about the cruelty of the past and how the landlord had mistreated the peasants. This kind of indoctrination, repeated day after day, reinforced the belief that life under the Communist Party leadership was the best in the world and that it was our duty as soldiers to preserve the system.

All of these traditions were intended to foster in us a sense of honor at being revolutionary soldiers; to fan our hatred of class enemies; and to teach us restraint, self-sacrifice, and obedience to the Party and the needs of the revolution.

It had a powerful effect. For instance, in the 1970s China and the Soviet Union sent high-range artillery and guided missile units to Vietnam to support the Vietcong. During an American bombing raid it was discovered that the Chinese artillery had too short a range and could not reach the bombers. Destruction over the target area was intense. Despite the ineffectiveness of their weapons, the Chinese soldiers continued to fire upward at the American planes, shouting quotations from Mao: "Be firm in resolve, don't fear sacrifice, push aside all difficulties, fight for victory!"

The Soviet guided missile units nearby stared at this with jaws dropping, doubtless thinking that their Chinese colleagues had lost their minds.

And during the days in Tienanmen, once again the soldiers did not complain. They obediently drove forward, aimed, and opened fire on command. In light of their training, how could it have been otherwise?

It is interesting, as I sit here in my study in the United States, to think of those soldiers in the square. Many of the protesters that the soldiers faced had themselves been soldiers and received Army training. I believe it was precisely that Army experience that allowed the demonstrators in and around Tienanmen to be so effective in disabling more than 1,000 of the military vehicles that appeared on the streets of Beijing.

When people in the West ask how I feel about the events in Tienanmen Square and the future of China, I am inevitably confronted with the contradiction between repulsion at the political blindness of the troops and the shedding of blood, and the deep affection I have for my time in the military and my life with my comrades. Rage at the soldiers who fought against unarmed protesters is mixed with comprehension of their reflex to obey.

What of my old father, the general? To this day our love is intact even though he still approves of the way the events in the square were handled, making the subject taboo between us. You ask me about China and I will tell you it is as complex as the emotions of a man sent to the fields to do hard labor for crimes he didn't commit, all the while approving of the decision to punish him since it was made by the Party. As complex as a son who wanted nothing more than to serve, but who found that service in challenging the old to bring about the new.

Translated by Jay Sailey

A LINE IN THE SAND

SAND

FR. KEVIN DOWLING

Photo by Togue Uchida

F r. Kevin Dowling was born in Savannah, Georgia. He attended the University of Tennessee at Chattanooga, where he received a B.S. in mathematics. He then entered St. Meinrad Seminary, where he received a Master's degree in Divinity. In 1980 he was ordained. He was commissioned an Air Force chaplain in 1984 and has served in that capacity since that time.

In early September 1990 his unit was mobilized and sent to Saudi Arabia, one of the first Air Force units sent to the Persian Gulf as part of Operation Desert Shield. His dispatches from the Gulf have appeared in the Nashville *Banner*.

Fr. Dowling lives in Loretto, Tennessee, where he is the pastor of Sacred Heart Church.

I had no sooner changed out of my vestments than I was called to the phone. My commander himself gave me the word: We were being deployed in support of Operation Desert Shield, the code name for the defense of Saudi Arabia against further Iraqi aggression. I had thirty-six hours to pack, he said. In my six years as an Air Force chaplain, this was the first time I had been told to prepare for service abroad. Of course, rumors had circulated that we might be mobilized when, on August 2, 1990, Iraq had invaded Kuwait. But already a few weeks had passed without any word from our officers.

Thirty-six hours turned into an unexplained wait of two weeks. In military operations secrecy leaves lots of people in the dark along the chain of command. When it's effective, snags that can't be explained for security reasons just look like confusion. Even I, schooled in patience, felt the tension of being suspended without a specific mission.

When the day of departure finally arrived, I took care of one last item that I had been putting off: I got myself a military haircut. The barber was an old World War II veteran. I went in to make his day.

"What can I do for you, Father?" he asked.

"I'm leaving for the Middle East tonight."

"Them's fightin' words." He stood erect, even the gray hairs on his balding head seeming to stand at attention. Then he licked his lips and stripped my head barer than a desert.

On my arrival at the base the commander took one look at me and exclaimed, "Chaplain, you look like a killer!" That was far from how I felt as I looked at the soldiers preparing to ship out with me. Wives, kids, girlfriends, and parents stood tearfully around their soldier, seizing the last minute for an embrace, a word of encouragement, an exchange of small items to be remembered by. This was a first for all of them, and the emotions were hard to deal with. Concern for family only added to each man's anxieties and doubled the pain. At a moment like that even a priest is not certain what word of solace to offer.

We took off, putting distance between us and our mundane concerns and freeing our focus for the future. The adventure was beginning.

I awoke on the floor of the plane as we made a sharp banking turn. From the window I could see nothing but yellow sand, an endless barren desert that welcomed no living thing.

The expression on the faces of my fellow soldiers reflected my own thoughts: We were a long way from Tennessee. Saddam Hussein had not endeared himself to us. Some moments later as I banged my head deplaning, my feelings about him were even less charitable. Iraq's strongman had just inflicted the first bit of damage. With my head pounding and my eyes blinded by the relentless sun, I stepped onto the tarmac. The whole base had come out to meet us—all twenty-two of them. It was clear that we had been sent to make one of the Pentagon's colored pushpins a reality.

We were certainly in the desert. The temperature was a blistering 115°F—cool, we were told, compared to the 135°F heat of a month before.

Air conditioned tents, over one hundred of them, in fact, had been set up on the apron of the runway by teams of engineers who had preceded us. The tents were of double thickness for insulation and had electrical outlets for lights, radios, and even microwave ovens. The air conditioning units ran day and night, and every four units had their own gasoline-powered generator. Thus the tents were kept at a comfortable 70°F, and at night we slept in arctic sleeping bags. Power cables snaked throughout the tent area. The main power unit was a huge German-made generator. Its hot exhaust was a sirocco turned blow-dryer, conveniently located outside the showers. The more patient, of course, could have their hair dried naturally in thirty seconds in the sun.

Air conditioning was not the only piece of technology that our commanders thought we might need in the desert. The full extent of their consideration was evident in the supplies we carried in. My first settling in consisted of unpacking five large duffel bags of clothing, chemical warfare suits, combat gear, and chapel supplies.

Each soldier had been issued three chemical warfare suits, each consisting of rubber boots, pants, top, gloves, mask, and hood. The mask has the look of a grasshopper head, conjuring up ominous thoughts of another plague, which only fed the fear of the plague looming over us in the form of poison gas. The mask contains two charcoal filters that detoxify all gases—except, we found out later, for the latest version in the Iraqi arsenal, which actually eats charcoal. A nozzle embedded in the mesh snugly fits into a special fixture on our canteens to allow us to drink water. The ensemble includes a decontamination kit. It contains paper that changes color in the presence of certain gases to help identify the threat; treated pads to wipe away blister agents that burn the skin; and cartridges of nerve-gas antidote that was to be injected into the upper leg in case of exposure.

During our regular monthly drills we had always dreaded chemical warfare training because it meant getting tear gas in our eyes. Each soldier was assigned his own personal gas mask. Soldiers with glasses were to have masks outfitted with lenses matching their prescription because the masks could not accommodate glasses. Contact lenses were ruled out because foreign substances could get between them and the eyes. We joked about chemical training because we thought such a threat existed only in the dreams of the Pentagon. Our instructors were always very serious and professional in their pre-sentations, but they never succeeded in convincing us that the training would ever be needed. I wonder now if even they believed it.

When I had gone to check out my gear before we were deployed, I had asked about the masks with prescription lenses, since my glasses are as thick as Coke bottles. The sergeant told me they couldn't be managed right now and to make the best of it.

We all tried to make the best of it. America goes to war the way Junior goes to college. I had brought along a ghetto blaster and a bag of cassettes under the guise of music for church services, but every night our tent swayed to champagne jazz. My forty-book library was tucked into the chemical warfare bag, along with a large bottle of wine for religious services disguised in a grape juice bottle. Moslem law prohibits alcohol, priests, and Christian services, but the Saudis made allowance for "spiritual advisers" as long as we were discreet. If caught with the grape juice bottle I intended to blame any fermentation on their ruinous desert heat.

As our home base built up, more conveniences were added. Pretty soon it was a small town, with a chow hall, beer tent, movie house, laundry service, and showers—not to mention a chapel. No brag, just fact—and all, we hoped, out of missile range, to protect the planes.

And, of course, our well-being was not merely in the hands of our commanders. A Bedouin trader called Crazy Abdul ran a quick-stop off the base that had everything from batteries and Coca-Cola to pita bread and Arab head coverings. He had built up a lucrative trade with us when an Indian trader who worked with our caterers saw a need and opened a store right on the base. Ice cream and midnight snacks became available. Merely a hint about a product was enough for this shrewd businessman to have a shipment arrive on the next truck. Postcards specifying our exact location were pulled by the commander as classified material, and no alcohol could be sold. However, the base beer tent allowed two beers per person per night.

The Air Force enjoyed better conditions all around than those of the forward-deployed infantry and Marines. The infantry were dug in in foxholes in dangerous proximity to the enemy, with showers rare, movies nonexistent, and food bad. The differences were the result of the separate military branches, their missions, and their ways of operating.

The site of our base was an ancient oasis on the caravan routes in the middle of Arabia. Deserts are known for mirages, and the base was a mirage in the making. Eight years earlier the Saudi government had leveled a square mile out of the shifting sand dunes for an airport to serve a city ten miles away. They had crushed an entire mountain and imported the rock as filler for a ten-inch bed over the sand floor. The shell of a terminal was the only building in sight, and it could have passed as easily for a building coming down as for one going up.

Crazy Abdul laughed at the project, saying it wasn't even needed. But the sheik's 747 was all the justification required for such a project in a monarchy. Before our arrival the sheik's plane was the only occupant of the airport. Pakistani mercenaries camped out around the plane day and night guarding it. (Only 20 percent of the inhabitants of Arabia are native Arabs; the other 80 percent are foreigners—Pakistanis, Indians, Iranians, Libyans—brought in to work.) The Pakistani guards had orders to shoot to kill if any of our soldiers took photos of His Majesty's plane.

The plane was complete, no doubt, with certain luxury

features, but it was also equipped with a compass constantly pointing to Mecca so that in flight the sheik could pray toward that holy city five times a day as do all good Moslems.

The sheik was also an avid horse and camel breeder and racer. Five figures was not an uncommon price to pay for an Australian camel, and the sheik was known to have transported his camels in a small stable in the plane. Horses, apparently, do not fly with as good grace as camels.

But the sheik was not the only one who needed the airport. We did, too. Our C-130 transport planes carried cargo throughout the theater. Passengers, heavy machinery, bombs, food, and mail were among the most common items aboard. To keep a number of such planes flying requires substantial manpower in flight crew, cargo handlers, air traffic controllers, maintenance personnel, avionics engineers, military police, operations officers to coordinate the whole flow, administration, and various areas of support one step removed from operations such as cooks, chaplains, and hospital staff. Our base, then, was home to all these people. And, like a mirage, we had designed it all so that it appeared we didn't exist.

This state of nonexistence operated not only as a tactic against our enemies but as a necessary strategem for our friends. As strangers in a strange land, we were reminded to be sensitive to the customs of our hosts. Girl-watching and drinking (what soldiers do best) were not allowed. When we visited town or went driving between bases we were instructed to look as much as possible like British tourists. We wore civilian dress so as not to alert terrorists to our identity. From all accounts of credit card activity, I believe we succeeded very well at acting out this role. This was a delight to the local merchants, whose bargains in gold and perfume were especially prized by us. However, I don't think I succeeded in looking like a Londoner, or any kind of Englishman for that matter. That World War II barber had quashed my chances there.

The success of our efforts to blend in can be seen in a contest we held to name the base. The winning entry was an Arabic term that means both "goodwill" and "God's will," but Arab neighbors informed us that it would be an insult to connect God in any way with something so common as land or soil. Even further, the contest was canceled when those same friends said that the notion of a named base implied a permanent installation in their land, which was not acceptable. Like a mirage, we were there but not really there. That was okay with us, too; it summed up the way we all felt: We were there, but our minds and hearts were miles away. Our thoughts were constantly of home.

*   *   *

The foulest verb in the military lexicon is "desert." It means "to abandon," and in the godforsaken sands of Arabia we felt that meaning firsthand.

Crossing the Egyptian desert and then the southern tip of the Sinai Peninsula, our journey to the desert recalled Moses and the Israelites and later the early Christian fathers who went into the desert to do spiritual battle. The western desert of the Arabian peninsula has mountainous beginnings at the Red Sea and declines to the more familiar dunes of the east near the Persian Gulf.

Islam itself was forged in the desert and, together with the desert connections of Judaism and Christianity, gives some plausibility to Renan's view that monotheism is the "natural religion of the desert." The character of the desert as a place of abandonment is the very quality conducive to spiritual encounter. From Moses on Mt. Sinai, "Take off your shoes, for the ground on which you stand is holy," to Jesus' response to the Devil, "Man does not live by bread alone," to John the Baptist, "I must decrease and he must increase," the desert has been an arena for stripping away

149

both the pretensions and the preservations of human life. The blinding sun, the burning heat, the dry air blown into a stinging whip of sand, the parched earth without flora, the cloudless days that never threaten rain conspire to make us feel our own mortality.

The Arabs who live in the desert adapt to it. They are nomadic because they understand that to survive in the desert means to shift with the sands. American forces arrived with a different conception of time and place: We came with the notion of a line drawn in the sand, a border that could not be violated without consequences.

We came to the desert not stripped to a minimum but fully equipped, our encounter with the desert buffered by technology and creature comforts. Showers with running hot and cold water call to mind the Bible's "streams in the desert." Coke cans printed in Arabic and English give us confidence that everything is going our way. But then there is the thought that our measure will be measured back to us: Our weapons of destruction may be used on us.

Standing outside my tent watching the sandstorm grind against the windshields of our C-130s, I couldn't help but shudder at the thought that we were on a dry run for the end of the world.

VLADEK AND THE CLOWN

PIOTR STASINSKI

P iotr Stasinski was born in Warsaw, Poland. He attended the University of Warsaw, where he received an M.A. in Polish Literature. He received a Ph.D. in Literary Theory from the Institute of Literary Research at the Polish Academy of Sciences in 1980.

Mr. Stasinski wrote for and edited underground Solidarity publications throughout the 1980s, when the union was banned. He also organized Solidarity activities during that period. The following two-part selection is drawn from the author's experience.

He has published a book, *The Poetics and Pragmatics of Feuilleton: The Theory and History of a Genre*. His articles have been published in several periodicals, including *Uncaptive Minds* and *Nowy Dziennik* in the United States and *Teksty, Pamietnik Literacki, Almanach Humanistyczny, Kultura Niezalezna, Wola*, and *Res Publica* in Poland. He is currently a journalist at the *Polish Daily News*.

Mr. Stasinski lives in New York with his wife and two children.

Vladek

His mother called when I was in the midst of one of those opposition paper undertakings that we students in the mid-seventies had to make time for to clear our precious souls of the swampy smell of communism's decadence and to clear our vicious bodies—of too much booze.

She said shyly that Vladek had asked for me to visit him in the hospital and would I be so kind as to get him a few new books, since he had nothing to read there. It was a military hospital.

I took a couple of titles from my own shelves, which those days had no chance to get dusty. They were a new African novel translated into Polish, the latest book by Garcia Marquez, a new edition of Franz Kafka's letters. At that time I was still struggling through the period of prolonged adolescence in which reading substituted for experience. It is common in my country. There has always been a shortage of housing, so college students had to live with their parents. As if their umbilical cords remained uncut, growing ever more tense; dried up and sterile long ago, but still there—stretched and poised to strangle either party. When they finally break, it's a violent act, leaving both the young and the old deeply hurt, especially "kids" unprepared to go on their own.

Before he quit the university and therefore immediately was drafted into the army, Vladek had lived with his serene mother and absent-minded father, always preoccupied with his various hobbies, and a few cats that made their tiny apartment stink with ammonia. I recalled that smell while entering the hospital, or rather my nose did.

A soldier filled out a pass for me and told me where to go. Another soldier, armed with a Russian Kalashnikov, checked the pass and asked my name when I approached room 105. Then he stepped into the room after me and stood quietly by the door. Vladek was lying between clean sheets and blankets stamped with inventory marks (the army is a thrifty organization, we were always reminded). The room wasn't small, and two other boys stared silently at us from their beds. Vladek's face scarcely contrasted with the linen background, except for his eyes, surrounded by deep-brown spots.

"Hi. You look terrible," I said. "Like my father in Auschwitz. Remember the picture in my home?" I was referring to a portrait painted by a friend of my father's right after they had been freed from that Nazi concentration camp in May 1945.

"Sure," said Vladek. "If I were your father, I wouldn't leave it hanging on my wall, having in mind the aesthetic upbringing of my noble progeny."

"I reluctantly agree. That picture made me deaf to music, although my dad was a violin virtuoso in his teens. Still, your aesthetic education seems also to have had its faults. Specifically, I mean the cats' odor in your humble quarters, which probably made you insensitive to more subtle shades of blue. Moreover, the very fact of your now being where you are and who you are suggests some omissions in the aesthetic criteria with which you were provided."

We went on in this manner for some time. We probably considered it funny, or at least as alleviating the awkwardness of the situation. Then I reached into my bag for the books I had brought . . . "Hold on!" I heard from the door. Our warder moved up to us and ordered me to show the contents of the bag. He relaxed quickly when he saw it was only books.

Vladek was particularly pleased to receive the African novel; he had read reviews of it and expected that it would allow him to stay comfortably at an exotic distance from reality. That had always been his problem: maintaining a space between himself and what was viewed as real by simple minds. He would go out of his way, causing very real trouble all around, to avoid the sticky embrace of common sense.

After his call-up, the army had sent him to some seaside range, where he became famous for his swift mastery of radiotelegraphy. Thanks to his musical ear (he could cope with any instrument, although he had no formal mu. :al training), he was the fastest in his unit and later won the contest for the whole military district. Officers liked him; he was given furloughs other soldiers could only dream of. He used them to test new drinking patterns and to travel by train across the country. He never bought train tickets and never visited his parents. He kept in touch only with his cousin, who also didn't mind spending two or three nights drinking but who, more importantly, worked in the court and canceled all the fines issued to Vladek by train conductors who were actually very lenient.

But despite Vladek's success and flamboyant life-style, not easily attained in the military, he could not forget that he still had a year and a half of service to go. This very realization had brought him to that hospital bed where he could again display his characteristic florid sarcasms while holding an African novel in one weak hand.

I asked him what had happened, and he began to tell me a hardly comprehensible story about leaving the barracks one night; selling his uniform; riding trains over enormous distances; meeting all kinds of odd people; drinking, being robbed and beaten; being saved, accommodated, cured, and fed by some provincial Ophelia . . . and finally, with his film cut (as we say in Polish, meaning that he was suffering from alcoholic amnesia), being found by the military police in a mudpuddle near Warsaw. He had lain there for several hours, half suffocated, stuffed with barbiturates and full of alcohol; unconscious, in a state of collapse.

While speaking, Vladek seemed not at all surprised by

what he had managed to do and see during his runaway spree, but rather by the fact that he remembered nearly everything except for the immediate circumstances preceding his attempt to swim in the mudpuddle. He also couldn't recall whether he had been heading to or from Warsaw.

"In general, perhaps I should be satisfied with the amount of sheer absurdity I was able to perform with a little help from good people and gracious gods," he concluded. He was not grateful for his miraculous survival.

"What are you going to do now?" I asked. It was the stupidest question I could have come up with. Vladek immediately brushed it aside, saying that his intentions were "entirely irrelevant since the court-martial would be interested in them up to the point of my desertion and not a bit further." I asked what penalty he might face after his release from the hospital.

"First, I want to deserve the definition of a patient," said Vladek, smiling toward the soldier at the door. "To the full extent of doctors' patience," he added.

"Later, I am not sure, but the judge may add more years to my army service. Anyway, I am determined to treat incarceration as an artistic experience. Unless fellow inmates stretch my imagination too far. But the court, I don't know. It is not my circus nor my apes . . . "

That was one of his "idiosyncratic proverbs," as he used to call those fancy sayings. When I learned a few weeks later that Vladek had been sentenced to two years, I even started to write his "proverbs" down, asking friends if they remembered any others. I also wrote to the authorities at the prison on the Baltic coast, to which Vladek was transferred, for permission to send him some books. They responded that there were no grounds for it since "the facility is equipped with an abundant library to which inmates enjoy full access."

He did not rejoin the army after prison. He was released on parole and deemed incapable of military service because of a "personality deficiency." I never saw him again. Someone told me that he served another prison term for breaking into a liquor store where he stole only one bottle of vodka. Then he was said to be living near Warsaw with a girl and their little son in an apartment shared with her parents. Their living space for three was part of a room behind a wardrobe. Vladek didn't feel inconvenienced much because he worked in a cosmetics factory and got up early; he usually returned "home" after dark. My informant could not remember his saying a word worth mentioning.

Mathaeus

Mathaeus entered the Rakowiecka prison cell in Warsaw with a broad smile on his face and his attention happily directed toward the occupants. He had been arrested the day before when soldiers had stopped the city bus on which he was riding, forced all the passengers out, and searched their bags. In his rucksack they had found a pile of illegal political leaflets. A month earlier martial law had been declared in Poland, and anyone detained for antigovernment activity faced court-martial; if convicted (the "if" is rather frivolous here), the sentence was set at no less than three years in prison. Mathaeus' mood did not seem to reflect an awareness of that.

Mine, however, did. I had already been in the "can" for a week or so, having been caught on a midtown street carrying a typewriter; a briefcase full of underwear for an "interned"[*] friend of mine; and another briefcase contain-

---

[*] A form of police detention. No charges are filed against the person, who is held in prison for an arbitrary length of time.

ing 500 copies of the first issue of an underground newspaper. I had founded the newspaper a few days earlier and written nearly every word of it. As it happened, I was arrested by a soldier from the unit that had regularly provided the honor guard at the Tomb of the Unknown Soldier. With the declaration of martial law all such troops, and all those used to honor foreign leaders arriving at the airport, were ordered to regular patrol service in the streets. "My" soldier, I learned later, was rewarded with a week's leave for capturing me. When Mathaeus appeared in my cell in the main prison of the Ministry of the Interior, it was two days after my twenty-ninth birthday and I still couldn't get rid of my feelings of depression.

I looked up at him with disgust, suspecting that he would only add to all the absurdities I had recently encountered.

"Don't worry," he said, after I had made a less than enthusiastic introduction of the other prisoners. "Amnesty will come soon."

I asked how he could be so certain.

He shrugged. "In any case, I'm not going to go into summary," he said and showed me a stamped typewritten sheet of paper. It was a psychiatrist's certificate stating that Mathaeus had been under surveillance in a ward and had been diagnosed as having a serious condition, the exact name of which I wasn't able to repeat after a while. That was how I first learned that there was a way to escape summary procedure. Mathaeus had known it beforehand and had made the necessary arrangements.

Later Mathaeus taught me various other things, although I was older, married and with a child, earning my living and supposedly a more experienced and serious academic. But my secure existence had not prepared me for the wholesale deprivation of prison. Mathaeus did not have what I had, what characterized me as a reliable, if politically revolting, member of society: stability. I didn't have what he had: a spontaneous drive to freedom.

Soon I found that I not only liked him but also appreciated his anarchic charm and respected the integrity of his behavior. He did not allow security officers to interrogate him in their preferred manner: He never let them intimidate him and never even sat down while being questioned. He was summoned, as I was, every other day. He used to pace the room in front of the interrogating officer, chain-smoking and laughingly deciding which questions he was in the mood to answer. Eventually he stopped answering at all, citing his rights, or else claiming important moral reservations against the "indirect accusation of the highest authorities for creating conditions in which his alleged offense could take place." He would insist that the officer record his explanations verbatim; otherwise, he wouldn't sign the protocol.

Mathaeus also did not observe the rules imposed on inmates. Not out of anger or revenge; no, he disregarded them because he didn't like them. I used to theorize about the nonsensical rules and regulations that were created for the sole purpose of humiliating the prisoners. Mathaeus agreed—he was a philosophy student, after all—but he didn't seem to act upon theory in this case. He would not declare his human dignity after refusing to stand up when a guard entered the cell; he would simply laugh. He would yield only if a subsequent penalty threatened to affect the rest of us. He began our violation of the ban on communication with other cells. He never let himself be searched voluntarily; the guards had to use force. He exercised all his rights with utter precision. He was first to demand to see a copy of the prison statutes and to write complaints about prison conditions to the authorities.

In the beginning Mathaeus had the dubious honor of being interrogated by three high-ranking officers of the military police, a colonel and two majors. They were determined to verify their suspicion that poor Mathaeus had been setting up underground military training courses. "Who was behind this military college?" they would ask him. It was more than even his capricious sense of humor could bear; the whole charge was based upon one finding—a gas mask pulled out from under Mathaeus' bed by diligent agents during a search of his and his parents' apartment (Mathaeus and his young wife, a teacher, occupied one tiny room there).

Mathaeus had actually found the mask in a garbage dump, but for some time he chose to play with the idea of a military college in front of the deadly serious investigators. They finally gave up, however, when he informed them that both the gas mask and the orders to establish clandestine military training had been given to him by a top Politburo official, Stefan Olszowski, in a covert attempt to undermine the country's current military leadership.

We used to play chess for hours, and when we did the stories would flow. Not only did Mathaeus have a talent for storytelling, he was also visibly delighted by some of the juicier details he recalled. I soon came to understand that the army was one of the chief inspirations for his life-art, his "school of pure nonsense," as he used to call it. Since he was not familiar with the book, I wrote to my family and asked them to send me *Catch-22*, the novel by Joseph Heller. I had to wait for it a whole month, so he had told me almost all of his stories by the time the book finally arrived. We then employed it as a manual for maintaining a sound mind under the stress of prison.

Mathaeus had served in the army for two full years because he had failed to register in time at the university. In the crucial year he had started his holidays too early and ended them too late. He returned home to find the call-up letter awaiting him. He faced the prospect of two violent years. Everyone who knew him had no doubt.

Defying his superiors and their orders was the easiest part of his inexhaustible industriousness as a soldier. He would spend weeks in solitary confinement or confined to barracks (for a change), interrupted by only short periods of regular duty. His refusal to participate in elections, which was compulsory for soldiers, cost him one particularly long period of confinement and gained him a reputation as an incorrigible subversive. However, he earned his fame as a permanent revolutionary by his jocular nonchalance rather than by vengeful doggedness.

Mathaeus had already been deprived of the right to carry arms when he was given a last opportunity to challenge the supreme absurdity of the military. The opportunity was provided by the commander of his unit, who still naively believed in the beneficial effects of penalizing Private Mathaeus.

The captain summoned Mathaeus and a fellow soldier who had fallen under his troublesome influence and ordered them to clean the company operations room completely. Mathaeus couldn't resist the temptation to confront the military hierarchy with simple logic. The order was carried out quite literally—completely. Left alone to do their work, the soldiers stretched blankets on the floor, piled up everything that happened to furnish the room, wrapped the stuff up and took it away to a garbage container in the yard. Undisturbed, they managed to remove maps, a library of instruction books, a choice collection of Marxist-Leninist classics, stationery, and all of the captain's utensils. They disassembled and removed lamps from the ceiling and a radio from the wall. They carried out everything in sight. After removing the last piece of furniture, they swept the room and started the most ambitious task: removing a huge, heavy safe from the corner. The captain discovered them as they were struggling with it. "We've almost cleared the mess, sir," Mathaeus reported.

One can only imagine the pandemonium that followed.

Mathaeus stubbornly insisted that he had executed the order to the letter. Knowing him, I could guess that he hadn't even tried to smile. He had been too tired.

Soon thereafter he was discharged. The army, with a sigh of relief, let him go, failing to add his days of arrest to the regular term of service. Mathaeus returned to Warsaw and entered the philosophy department at the university.

After a couple of weeks in the same prison cell, we were separated. It was too much for our oppressors, who felt, presumably, that their task of "resocializing" us could not be fulfilled. We had already been filing one daily complaint each. The complaints were identical in content, but there were always two of them since it was prohibited to file jointly.

Any joint action was strictly forbidden. Therefore we communicated with other cells almost every night, either by using a toilet (you only had to keep it clean and remove water from the bowl before speaking into it; this communication system linked six cells at once), or simply by shouting through the cell windows. Among many other things, we had demanded religious services for an as yet nonexistent creed: Judaislamism, which we wanted to create in an effort to end the centuries-old hostility between Jews and Arabs. Our idealism was not appreciated by the flat-minded, uniformed bureaucrats.

We then embarked upon a serious protest action that involved extensive preparation. We started to "print" leaflets, using aluminum foil (food parcels from families), ink blown out from a ball-point pen and mixed with face cream, paper, and a needle. The needle was critical to our technology. We obtained it from guards (you were allowed to sew a button on your prison fatigues). When they gave a needle to an inmate they used to hang a notice on the cell door saying, "Needle inside," and they retrieved it after an hour. That was time enough to perforate a text on the foil, making a stencil. The leaflets we manufactured in this manner called upon other political prisoners to join in the singing of patriotic songs on the thirteenth day of the following month—to commemorate the day martial law had been imposed.

The protest failed despite the fact that we had been able to make about 100 leaflets. The guards started to pick them up off the ground in the concrete wells that served as our exercise areas (half an hour each day). We were frisked before and after our walks, and when we were outside the guards searched our cell. They never found anything and so decided to break this subversive plot in another way.

Mathaeus was dragged from our cell and was moved into the cell block next to ours. He immediately declared a hunger strike, and some milky cereal, called "gypsum," was forced down his throat every day. I also learned that he was beaten and later sent to the prison hospital ward. He maintained his hunger strike while there, even though forced feeding amounted to regular torture.

We met a long time after he had been released (he spent a few months more in Rakowiecka than I did). I was again busy with my underground newspaper, and he became involved in a clandestine printing group. Once again, the army and prison were our natural topics of conversation.

"The army is worse," Mathaeus maintained. "In prison, especially if you are a political, they don't try to use you or to change you into someone else. Army is worse. They never rest until they have driven you mad: You must be either a servant or a clown. Whatever they can do to you, they'll do. Remember?"

Glossary

aggro – short for aggression
Bessbrook – a town in Northern Ireland
Crossmaglen (kros mə glen') – a town on the border between Northern Ireland and Ireland
gerontocracy – a government ruled by elderly leaders
glasnost (gläs'nost) – governmentally sanctioned freedom for leaders and citizens alike to speak honestly about the problems and the prospects for the Soviet Union.
hummus (hum'us) – Middle Eastern dish made from crushed chick peas
IRA – Irish Republican Army
kaffiyeh (kə fē'ə) – Arab cotton cloth headdress
Kalashnikov (kə läsh'ni kof) – a type of Soviet-made rifle
kasbah (kaz'bä) – business district in an Arab town
kibbutznik (ki bŏŏts'nik) – settler on an Israeli collective farm (kibbutz)
lino – short for linoleum
lorry – truck
Marxists – adherents to the philosophies of Karl Marx (1818–1883), whose doctrines are the basis of modern socialism
May Day – May 1, an international labor holiday, observed in many countries by parades or demonstrations
muezzin (myŏŏ ez'in) – Moslem town crier who calls people to prayer
paddies – a derogatory name for the Irish
PLO – Palestine Liberation Organization
Royal Ulster Constabulary – the police force in Northern Ireland
Saigon – the capital of South Vietnam
shekel (shek'əl) – an Israeli coin
tahini (tə hē'nē) – dip made from crushed sesame

Bibliography

Afghanistan:

Girardet, Edward. *Afghanistan: The Soviet War*. New York: St. Martin's Press, 1985. A historical account of the early years of the Soviet occupation, this book details why the invasion was so easy, how the war was fought, and how life was lived in the embattled nation.

Borovik, Artem. *The Hidden War: A Russian Journalist's Account of the Soviet War in Afghanistan*. New York: The Atlantic Monthly Press, 1990. A look at the war from the point of view of Soviet soldiers, this book documents the frustration, anger, and terror felt by those sent to fight in Afghanistan.

China:

Liu Binyan, Ruan Ming, and Xu Gang. *"Tell the World": What Happened in China and Why*. New York: Pantheon, 1990. An incredible eyewitness account of the uprisings in China and the accompanying leadership struggle, and a discussion of the current crisis.

Shen Tong and Marianne Yen. *Almost a Revolution*. New York: Houghton Mifflin, 1990. An insider's account of the uprising and crackdown of June 1989, this book is a personal look at the extraordinary day-to-day events.

Spence, Jonathan D. *The Search for Modern China*. New York: W.W. Norton & Co., 1990. The author uses fiction, poetry, and folk song to paint a vivid picture of China's past and present. This highly acclaimed book examines the links between the modern struggles for power and the struggles of China's past.

Israel:

Grossman, David. *The Yellow Wind*. New York: Farrar, Straus and Giroux, 1988. An Israeli journalist's account of time spent in the occupied West Bank, the book offers a close-up view of the daily life of the Palestinians in the region.

O'Brien, Conor Cruise. *The Siege*. New York: Simon and Schuster, 1986. This insightful book traces the history of the Jewish state. Beginning with the late nineteenth century, the author discusses the struggles, dilemmas, triumphs, and failures in the effort to create a secure nation.

Lebanon:

Friedman, Thomas L. *From Beirut to Jerusalem*. New York: Farrar, Straus and Giroux, 1989. An account of life in the two cities by an Arabic-speaking American journalist who worked for nine years in the region.

Glass, Charles. *Tribes with Flags*. New York: The Atlantic Monthly Press, 1990. An account of the chaos of the Middle East by an ABC correspondent who was kidnapped in Beirut and later managed an incredible escape.

Makdisi, Jean Said. *Beirut Fragments: A War Memoir*. New York: Persea, 1990. This book examines the war in Beirut and the international indifference to the national tragedy that is Lebanon. The writer is a native of Beirut.

Lithuania:

Milosz, Czeslaw. *The Issa Valley*. New York: Farrar, Straus and Giroux, 1981. Written by a native of Lithuania, this novel tells of a young boy's experiences in a secluded, backward Lithuanian town.

Motyl, Alexander. *Sovietology, Rationality, Nationality: Coming to Grips with Nationalism in the USSR*. New York: Columbia University Press, 1990.

Nicaragua:

Cabezas, Omar. *Fire from the Mountain: The Making of a Sandinista*. The author, a high-ranking member of the

Sandinista leadership, tells the story of his involvement in the Nicaraguan revolution. Cabezas gives a personal account of what it means to be involved in guerrilla warfare.

Crawley, Eduardo. *Nicaragua in Perspective.* New York: St. Martin's Press, 1984, rev. ed. A history of Nicaragua and its people from the time of colonization to the first years of the Sandinista government.

Meiselas, Susan (edited by Claire Rosenberg). *Nicaragua: June 1978 to July 1979.* New York: Pantheon, 1981. Photographs of Nicaragua in the twelve months leading up to the revolution and the overthrow of the Somoza government.

Northern Ireland:

Belfrage, Sally. *Living with War; A Belfast Year.* New York: Sifton Books, 1987. The author reports on a year she spent in Northern Ireland, during which she spoke with numerous people representing most of the groups involved in the conflict.

Renwick, Aly. . . . *last night another soldier* . . . Nottingham: The Russel Press, 1989. A novel set in West Belfast, it tells the stories of two young people, a Scottish soldier and a republican, caught up in the dramatic early years of "the troubles."

Poland:

Davies, Norman. *God's Playground, A History of Poland: Vol. 1 and 2.* New York: Columbia University, 1982. A comprehensive history of Poland.

Konwicki, Tadeusz. *The Polish Complex.* New York: Farrar, Straus and Giroux, 1982. A novel that was banned in Poland for its all-too-candid portrayal of life under an oppressive government.

Saudi Arabia/Iraq:

Mackey, Sandra. *The Saudis: Inside the Desert Kingdom.* New

York: Houghton Mifflin, 1987. The author used her position as the wife of an American doctor in Saudi Arabia as a cover for investigative reporting. She discusses the effects of modernization on the traditional culture, the role of women, Islam, the Bedouins, the royal family, and other interesting subjects.

Miller, Judith, and Mylroie, Laurie. *Saddam Hussein and the Crisis in the Gulf.* New York: Times Books/Random House, 1990. A *New York Times* reporter and a scholar explore the career of the Iraqi leader.

Vietnam:

Butler, Robert Owen. *On Distant Ground.* New York: Alfred A. Knopf, 1985. A novel about an American soldier tried for kidnapping and freeing a Vietcong prisoner, who goes back to Vietnam and confronts his past.

Wright, Stephen. *Meditations in Green.* New York: Charles Scribner's Sons, 1983. The story of a man's slow and shocking adjustment to living in a war and to life afterward.

Safer, Morley. *Flashbacks: On Returning to Vietnam.* New York: Random House, 1990. A television correspondent reflects on the war he covered for CBS.

Zimbabwe:

Frederikse, Julie. *None but Ourselves.* London: Heinemann, 1983. A collage of various sources and images that vividly portrays both sides of the struggle in Rhodesia that gave birth to independent Zimbabwe.

Moore-King, Bruce. *White Man, Black War.* London: Penguin, 1989. A soldier's riveting account of his participation in the Rhodesian conflict that led him to reject the values of the society for which he was forced to fight.

Index

A
Afghanistan, 3-8, 12-16
Air Force, United States, 143-150

B
bayonet, 7-8
Beijing, 131-132, 140
Border Patrol, Israeli, 34-35
British Army, 61-75

C
Chamorro, Violeta, 101
chaplain, U.S. Air Force, 143-150
chemical warfare, 145-146
children
    Irish, 65-75
    Lebanese, 115-127
    Nicaraguan, 82-91
    Palestinian, 29-41
China, Peoples's Republic of, 79-80, 131-140
civil war, Lebanese, 121-127
Communist Party, Chinese, 131, 139
comrade, death of 12-16, 73-74, 107, 126
conscription
    Polish Army, 153-163
    Soviet Army, 45-58
contras, Nicaraguan, 81-102
Crossmaglen, Northern Ireland, 61-75

D
dedovshchina, 47, 53
desert deployment, 144-150
desertion, from Soviet Army, 53-58
draft
    Polish military, 153

Soviet military, resistance to, 52-53
dream, of killing, 4-5
drinking, in Soviet Army, 47, 49
drug addiction, 12-14

E
El Salvador, 79

F
fear, childhood vs. adult, 19-20
Fedayee, 121
funeral, of Sandinista soldier, 95-98

G
glasnost, 46

H
helicopter, 61-64, 67-68, 74-75, 107

I
imprisonment, of Polish soldiers, 153-164
Iraq, 143
Irish Republican Army, 65, 71-75
Israel, 29-41, 116

J
Jinotega, Nicaragua, 86-87

K
kidnapping, of Lithuanian soldiers, 53-57
Kuwait, 143

L
La Penca, Nicaragua, 88-89, 92
Lebanon, 115-127
Lin Biao, 134

Index

Lithuania, 45-58

M
machine gun, 6-7, 14-16, 111
Managua, Nicaragua, 79-80
Mao Tse-tung, 134, 139
Matagalpa, Nicaragua, 98-99
Mazoe River, Rhodesia, 106-112
militia, Lebanese, 121-122, 125-126

N
Nanjing, China, 133-134
Nicaragua, 79-102
Northern Ireland, 61-75

O
Operation Desert Shield, 143-150
opium, 12-16

P
Palestine Liberation Organization,
    29, 35, 41, 116, 119, 121
Palestinians, 29-41
paratroopers, 54-55
patrolling
    of Northern Ireland, 65-75
    of occupied territories, 29-41
    of Rhodesia, 106-112
People's Liberation Army, 131-132
Poland, 153-163
prisoners of war, 4-8
prison, Polish, 153-163

R
Red Cross, Lithuanian, 45
Rhodesia, 105-112
Royal Ulster Constabulary, 64

S
Saigon, escape from, 24
Sajudis reform movement, 56
Sandinistas, 79-102
Saudi Arabia, 143-150
Shiites, 115-116, 120, 121
Shinbet, 32, 36-37, 40
Siauliai movement, 52
Sigitas, 47
soldiers
    American, 143-150
    British, 61-75
    Chinese, 131-140
    Israeli, 29-41
    Lithuanian, 45-58
    Nicaraguan, 82-98
    Polish, 153-163
    Rhodesian, 105-112
    Soviet, 2-8
    abuse by, 46-50
Soviet Union, 2-4, 45-58
suicide, 3, 50
Sunnis, 120, 121

T
tanks, 132
tear gas, 38
terrorism, 29, 65, 75
Tienanmen Square, 131-140
training, military, 84-86, 134-138

V
Vietnam
    myth of founding, 21-26
    war, 19-26, 139

Z
Zimbabwe African National
    Liberation Army, 106